# Theories of Educational Management

**Tony Bush** is Professor of Educational Management and Director of the Educational Management Development Unit at the University of Leicester. He was formerly a teacher in secondary schools and colleges and a professional officer with a local education authority. He was senior lecturer in educational policy and management at the Open University before joining Leicester in January 1992. He has published extensively on several aspects of educational management. His main recent books are *Directors of Education: Facing Reform* (1989) Jessica Kingsley (with M Kogan and A Lenney); *Managing Education: Theory and Practice* (1989), Open University Press; *Managing Autonomous Schools: The Grant Maintained Experience* (1993), (with M Coleman and D Glover), Paul Chapman and *The Principles of Educational Management* (1994), (with J West-Burnham) Longman.

# Theories of Educational Management

## Second Edition

### Tony Bush
UNIVERSITY OF LEICESTER

P·C·P
Paul Chapman
Publishing Ltd

Copyright © Tony Bush 1995

Paul Chapman Publishing Ltd
144 Liverpool Road
London
N1 1LA

British Library Cataloguing in Publication Data

Bush, Tony
    Theories of Educational Management
    2Rev.ed
    I. Title
    371.2001
    ISBN 1 85396 283 X

Typeset by Dorwyn Ltd, Rowlands Castle, Hants
Printed and bound by Athenæum Press Ltd., Gateshead

C D E F G H   9 8 7

# Contents

# Preface

The significance of good management for the effective operation of schools and colleges has been increasingly acknowledged during the 1980s and 1990s. The trend towards self-management in the United Kingdom and much of the English speaking world has led to an enhanced appreciation of the importance of managerial competence for educational leaders. The institution is now the prime unit in the local educational system and governing bodies, heads and principals have substantial responsibilities for the management of staff, finance and links with the community. The vitality, and perhaps the very survival, of schools and colleges depends on their ability to meet the needs of their current and potential clients.

The first edition of this book was published in 1986, before the seismic changes to the educational system engendered by the Education Reform Act and subsequent legislation. The shift to institutional management has been accompanied by tentative steps to develop the managerial competence of senior staff, particularly headteachers. The School Management Task Force (SMTF) set the agenda for management development in its 1990 report (SMTF 1990) but, unlike many other countries, there is still no requirement for management training for heads in the United Kingdom. Mentoring programmes exist for new headteachers and the 'Headlamp' scheme, introduced in 1995, provides an entitlement for training for new heads but no obligation for them to take part.

There are no national programmes for deputy heads or for other senior and middle managers in schools or colleges but there is considerable demand for accredited programmes at many universities in the United Kingdom. Anecdotal evidence suggests that it is now rare for teachers to obtain headships without first acquiring a master's degree or another advanced qualification in educational management. The control of substantial budgets, a concern for the welfare of staff and the need to ensure effective teaching and learning, all require high order managerial skills and understanding. Just as teachers require training to be effective in the classroom, so heads, principals and senior staff need training to be competent managers. Many factors contribute to differences in the performance of educational institutions but there is evidence that the quality of management is an important variable in distinguishing between successful and less successful schools.

There is now a substantial literature on management practice in educational organizations in response to the establishment of many new courses on educational management. However, there have been few attempts to address the theoretical foundations of good practice. The aim of this book is to provide some conceptual frameworks to guide the practice of educational managers. Since 1986 there has been some research linking theory to practice in schools and colleges and these studies are reflected in this volume. The author seeks to present a complex body of theory in clear, straightforward terms and to illustrate the models by reference to examples of management in educational institutions. In making relevant theory more accessible to practitioners, the intention is to promote both greater understanding of the concepts underpinning effective management practice and to develop the capability of senior and middle managers in schools and colleges.

Chapter 1 defines educational management and stresses the centrality of aims or goals in guiding managerial practice. The historical development of educational management as a distinct subject is chronicled from its dependence on industrial models in the 1960s to its position in the 1990s as an established discipline with an evolving specialist literature. The debate on whether education should be regarded as simply a different context for the application of general management principles, or a special case justifying a distinct approach, is also reflected in this chapter. The factors affecting the management of professional staff are considered and the chapter concludes with a reference to the issues involved in managing organizations in a 'wild' environment.

Chapter 2 considers the relationship between theory and practice. The prospect of a theory/practice divide can be avoided by an appreciation of the relevance of theory. The characteristics of educational management theory are discussed and the chapter also discusses the relationship between gender and theory.

The next six chapters are the heart of the book, each presenting one of the major models of educational management. The six perspectives are analysed in terms of the assumptions made about the goals of educational institutions, the nature of organizational structure, relations with the external environment and the most appropriate modes of leadership.

Chapter 3 considers formal models, with their emphasis on hierarchical structures, rational processes and official authority. Chapter 4 outlines the normatively preferred collegial model with its stress on the authority of expertise, the shared values and objectives of professional staff and decision-making based on consensus.

Chapter 5 presents political models with their assumptions of conflict between interest groups and of decisions dependent on the relative resources of power deployed by the various factions. Chapter 6 examines subjective models with their emphasis on individual interpretation of events and their rejection of the concept of organizational goals.

Chapter 7 discusses ambiguity models which stress the unpredictability of organizations, the lack of clarity about goals and the fluid nature of participation in decision-making. Chapter 8 is new and focuses on the increasingly important issue of organizational culture. This model emphasizes the values and beliefs in organizations and the symbols and rituals used to reinforce culture.

Chapter 9 compares the six models and considers their validity for particular types of school or college. The chapter considers several attempts to integrate some of the models and concludes by assessing how to use theory to improve practice.

I am grateful to the many people who have contributed to the development of this volume. I received valuable comments on a draft of the text from my former colleague Professor Ron Glatter of the Open University, Professor Les Bell of Liverpool John Moores University, Professor Peter Ribbins of Birmingham University and my University of Leicester colleagues Marianne Coleman, Derek Glover and John O'Neill. Alan Wray aided the preparation of the text by producing a detailed survey of the literature published since 1986. Felicity Murray made my task much easier by creating a word processed version of the first edition (originally produced on a typewriter!) and by her skilful administration of the project. Finally, I am grateful for the understanding of Beryl, Graham and Alison during the four month gestation period of this book.

Tony Bush
University of Leicester
November 1994

# 1

# *The Importance of Management for Education*

## What is educational management?

Educational management is a field of study and practice concerned with the operation of educational organizations. There is no single generally accepted definition of the subject because its development has drawn heavily on several more firmly established disciplines including sociology, political science, economics and general management: 'We are looking at a field of management studies characterized by a considerable flexibility of discipline boundaries' (Harries-Jenkins, 1984, p. 216). Interpretations drawn from different disciplines necessarily emphasize diverse aspects of educational management and these varying approaches are reflected in subsequent chapters of this book.

Many definitions of educational management are *partial*, reflecting the particular stance of their authors. Those which attempt a broader approach are often rather bland. Hoyle (1981, p. 8), for example, describes his definition as 'downbeat': 'Management is a continuous process through which members of an organisation seek to co-ordinate their activities and utilise their resources in order to fulfil the various tasks of the organisation as efficiently as possible.' Cuthbert (1984) suggests that management 'is an activity involving responsibility for getting things done through other people'.

Glatter's (1979, p. 16) definition is useful because it serves to identify the scope of the subject. He argues that management studies are concerned with 'the internal operation of educational institutions, and also with their relationships with their environment, that is, the communities in which they are set, and with the governing bodies to which they are formally responsible.' This statement delineates the boundaries of educational management but leaves open questions about the nature of the subject. What are those issues which are centrally the concern of a managerial approach to schools and colleges? Arguably, educational management has at its heart matters concerned with the purposes or aims of education.

Most writers on educational management emphasize the significance of purposes or goals in education. Culbertson (1983), for example, claims that 'defining purpose is a central function of administration'. Cyert (1975) argues that 'an organisation is developed to achieve certain goals or objectives by group activity'. The centrality of the goal orientation of schools and colleges is common to most of the different theoretical approaches to the subject. There is disagreement, though, about three aspects of goal-setting in education:

- the value of *formal* statements of purpose;
- whether the objectives are those of the organization or those of particular individuals;
- *how* the institution's goals are determined.

## Formal aims

The formal aims of schools and colleges tend to be set at a high level of generality. They usually command substantial support but, because they are often utopian, such objectives provide an inadequate basis for managerial action. A typical aim in a primary or secondary school might focus on the acquisition by each pupil of physical, social, intellectual and moral qualities and skills. This is worthy but it has considerable limitations as a guide to decision-making. More specific purposes often fail to reach the same level of agreement. A proposal to seek improved performance in the core curriculum of English, mathematics and science, for example, may be challenged by teachers concerned about the implications for foundation subjects. The emphasis on development planning in the 1990s provides a vehicle for resolving these dilemmas and determining school and college priorities.

## Organizational or individual aims

Some approaches to educational management are concerned predominantly with *organizational* objectives while other models strongly emphasize *individual* aims. There is a range of opinion between these two views. Gray (1979, p. 12), stresses both elements: 'the management process is concerned with helping the members of an organisation to attain individual as well as organisational objectives within the changing environment of the organisation.' A potential problem is that individual and organizational objectives may be incompatible or that organizational aims satisfy some, but not all, individual aspirations. It is reasonable to assume that most teachers want their school or college to pursue policies which are in harmony with their own interests and preferences. Coulson (1985, p. 44) is probably right to assert that 'the goals and motivations of all the individuals involved in the life of the school interpenetrate with the goals officially attributed to the organisation'.

## The determination of aims

The process of deciding on the aims of the organization is at the heart of educational management. In some settings, aims are decided by the headteacher, often working in association with the senior management team and a small group of lay governors. In many schools and colleges, however, goal setting is a corporate activity undertaken by formal bodies or informal groups.

School and college aims are inevitably influenced by pressures emanating from the wider educational environment. The arguments about the National Curriculum in England and Wales are symptomatic of the diverse views about the extent and nature of prescription over the content of education. Institutions may be left with the residual task of interpreting external imperatives rather than determining aims on the basis of their own assessment of student need. Alternatively, teachers may have to choose between conflicting external requirements:

> No curriculum would last beyond a week if teachers and managers took seriously the ever increasing flood of prescriptive advice offered by politicians and pressure groups. Thus the role of 'gate keeper' has fallen upon senior staff, who have to take on the uncomfortable but necessary task of selection.
>
> (Lofthouse, 1994, p. 145)

The nature of the goal-setting process is a major variant in the different models of educational management to be discussed in subsequent chapters.

## The chronology of educational management

The origins and development of educational management as a distinct discipline have been well chronicled by Culbertson (1980), Bone (1982), Hughes (1985) and Hughes and Bush (1991). It began in the United States in the early part of this century. The work of Taylor (1947) was particularly influential and his 'scientific management movement' is still subject to vigorous debate, particularly by those who oppose a 'managerial' approach to education. Another important contributor to management theory was the French writer Fayol (1916) whose 'general principles of management' are still significant. Weber's (1947) work on 'bureaucracy' remains powerful and this will be given extended treatment in Chapter 3.

All these theories developed outside education and were subsequently applied to schools and colleges, with mixed results. The other models discussed in this book were developed in the educational context or have been applied to schools or colleges in their formative periods.

The development of educational management as a field of study in the United Kingdom came as late as the 1960s but there has been rapid expansion since then. In 1983 the Department of Education and Science (DES) sponsored a programme of management training for heads and established the National Development Centre for School Management Training at Bristol University. University courses on school and college management became increasingly popular (Hughes, Carter and Fidler, 1981).

## The Education Reform Act

The scope and nature of management in schools and colleges changed dramatically in England and Wales with the implementation of the Education Reform Act (1988). This major reform was described by Maclure (1988, p. ix) as 'The most important and far-reaching piece of educational law-making . . . since the Education Act of 1944 . . . because it altered the basic power structure of the education system'. The legislation increased the powers of the Secretary of State and reduced the authority of the local education authorities (LEAs). It gave governing bodies and principals substantial discretion to manage their own schools and colleges, albeit within a framework of increased national control of the curriculum.

The Education Reform Act (ERA), and subsequent legislation, have transformed the educational landscape which is now very different from the pre-ERA scene. The major changes are as follows:

- The National Curriculum which specifies in considerable detail the content of the curriculum and the assessment arrangements for pupils at ages seven, eleven, fourteen and sixteen.
- Local Management of Schools (LMS) which devolves funding and resource management to governing bodies and school staff and greatly reduces the powers of the local educational authorities (LEAs).
- Open Enrolment which removes artificial limits on the capacity of schools and enables parents to choose the school their children will attend, subject only to its physical capacity. School budgets are linked closely to pupil numbers, encouraging schools to compete for pupils in order to sustain or increase their income.
- The provision for schools to 'opt out' of LEA control and become grant-maintained, receiving their revenue and capital budgets from a funding agency whose members are appointed by the Secretary of State for Education.
- The incorporation of further education colleges as autonomous bodies, independent of LEAs.
- The introduction of a nationally controlled inspection regime which will ensure that all schools are inspected once every four years according to criteria established by the Office for Standards in Education (OFSTED).

(Bush and West-Burnham, 1994, pp. 1–2)

## Self-management

These developments in England and Wales place schools and colleges at the heart of 'the educational market place' with students and parents as customers, choosing from a range of providers. This shift is paralleled by similar trends in much of the developed world. Caldwell and Spinks (1988; 1992) document this trend which they describe as 'self-management': 'A self-managing school is a school in a system of education where there has been significant and consistent decentralisation to the school level of authority to make decisions related to the allocation of resources' (Caldwell and Spinks, 1992, p. 4). The authors argue that self-management is now so widespread that it merits classification as an educational 'megatrend'. They expound the case for self-managing schools in these terms:

> It is simply more efficient and effective in the late twentieth century to restructure systems of education so that central bureaucracies are relatively small and schools are empowered to manage their own affairs within a

centrally determined framework of direction and support. Two arguments have usually been offered, one is concerned with responsiveness, the other with priorities for resource allocation in times of economic restraint or budgetary crisis.

(Caldwell and Spinks, 1992, p. 14)

Autonomous schools and colleges may be regarded as potentially more efficient and effective but much depends on the nature and quality of internal management if the putative benefits of autonomy are to be realized.

## School Management Task Force

The seismic change in the balance of power in education leaves governors and staff with the responsibility to control many aspects of school and college management which had previously been the preserve of the LEAs. However, it is evident that many heads and senior staff are inadequately prepared for their new responsibilities. Trained as teachers rather than managers, they have to acquire new skills if their schools are to thrive in the new climate of self-management.

The response of the then Department of Education and Science was to establish the School Management Task Force (SMTF). Its 1990 report was influential in setting the agenda for change but many of its recommendations have not been implemented. The report refers to the training needs of 130,000 senior or middle managers in primary and secondary schools and points to the oddity of appointing heads without management training:

Given heads' high and increasing level of responsibility, it is perhaps surprising that candidates for headship are required to have no specific training, no minimum length of service and no other qualification other than to teach; this is in contrast to a number of other countries where successful completion of management training courses . . . [is] laid down in law.

(SMTF, 1990, p. 3)

The DFE has subsequently sponsored mentoring for new heads to enable them to benefit from the experience of more established heads. It also plans to implement the 'Headlamp' scheme for the management development of new heads in 1995. However, it has not prescribed or recommended training for aspiring heads to establish their suitability *before* appointment. In practice, though, many senior managers now have master's degrees in educational management or related subjects and it is increasingly difficult to obtain headships without evidence of management training. Leicester University's MBA in Educational Management, which has more than 600 participants, is one example of the increasing interest in management development for education professionals.

The growth of educational management as a distinct discipline reflects the view that the management of educational institutions is enhanced by training just as teachers require training to be effective in the classroom. The content and nature of training for educational management is more contentious. In particular there is disagreement about whether the management of education is different from the management of other organizations.

## The significance of the educational context

Educational management as a field of study and practice was derived from management principles first applied to industry and commerce, mainly in the United States (see page 3). Theory development largely involved the application of industrial models to educational settings. As the subject became established as an academic discipline in its own right, its theorists and practitioners began to develop alternative models based on their observation of, and experience in, schools and colleges. By the mid-1990s the main theories, featured in this book, have either been developed in the educational context or have been adapted from industrial models to meet the specific requirements of schools and colleges.

Educational management has progressed from being a new field dependent upon ideas developed in other settings to become an established discipline with its own theories and some empirical data testing their validity in education. This transition has been accompanied by lively argument about the extent to which education should be regarded as simply another field for the application of general principles of management or be seen as a separate discipline with its own body of knowledge.

*The 'general principles' argument*   One strand of opinion asserts that there are general principles of management which can be applied to all organizational settings:

> Schools have much in common with other organisations that bring people together for a purpose – be they hospitals, or businesses or government offices.
>
> (Handy, 1984, p. 26)

> The assertion that every enterprise represents a unique case which calls for its own solution is without foundation and contradicted by the facts.
>
> (Haag, 1982, p. 33)

Walker (1984, p. 20) advocates common management education for administrators from government, business and education. He believes that 'these men and woman learn from one another in a process of managerial symbiosis'.

The case for a common approach to the training and development of managers rests largely upon the functions thought to be common to different types of organization. These include financial management, human resource management and relationships with the organization's clients and the wider community.

Squire (1987, p. 1) strongly advocates the application of general management principles to education and asserts that

> The education service is managed in a mode which is seriously defective . . . the service needs urgently to fight a battle of competence in management if this skew is to be corrected . . . Education management should be seen as a distinctive mode of management rather than as a substantive, radically distinguishable activity.

Squire appears to argue that educational management is defective because of its 'resistance to management theory' (p. 31) in general and in particular in its rejection of Management by Objectives (MBO), a technique which has been largely discredited in industry. The empirical basis for his arguments is flimsy.

West-Burnham's (1994, pp. 19–20) more measured approach examines seven 'differences' between educational and general management and concludes that these are based on false assumptions about the nature of industrial management. 'Critics of management in education rarely cite specific texts or examples of management practice. Management theory is usually found to be derived from Fayol or Taylor and "practice" is usually anecdotal . . . . Great care is needed to avoid debating the nature of educational management using stereotypical and false premises.'

*The 'special case' argument*   The majority view among academics and practitioners is that the management of educational institutions is sufficiently different to merit separate provision for the development of school and college managers:

> Educational institutions differ along crucial dimensions from other kinds of organisations . . . training for educational administrators should predominantly be provided in relation to their particular area of managerial activity.
> (Glatter, 1972, pp. 8–9)

> Management theory and practice have been developed mainly in connection with industrial and commercial activities, which are seen as intrinsically different from the activities of educational institutions.
> (Taylor, 1976, p. 41)

> Scholars are questioning the fruitfulness of building or relying upon general theories of administration . . . such an orientation, they argue, leads inevitably to the neglect of educational purpose and practice and the special features of leadership and change in educational institutions.
> (Culbertson, 1980, p. 327)

> Teachers . . . are often impatient when they hear about line management in schools. They see it as an inappropriate attempt to introduce industrial techniques into a situation which is based on personal relationships. Education, they say, is not susceptible to the imposition of hard-headed business concepts designed to increase profit margins.
> (Barrell, 1982, p. 6)

Al-Khalifa (1986) refers to the differences between public and private sector organisations and challenges the notion of 'generic' management:

> The treatment of non-educational management as generic is in itself unsatisfactory when it is recalled that a variety of organizations are included in this . . . If comparison between public and private sector services is seen to be difficult then arguably it must be even more so in the case of schools.
> (Al-Khalifa, 1986, p. 237)

There are seven major ways in which the management of educational institutions differs markedly from the management of other organizations:

1. The *objectives* of educational institutions, in common with those of many other service organizations, are much more difficult to define than the purposes of commercial companies. There are no clear-cut educational

equivalents to the main private sector objectives such as profit maximization, output maximization or product diversification. Schools and colleges are expected to develop the personal capacity of individuals, to inculcate the accepted values and beliefs, to look after children and young people for set periods of each day and to prepare pupils and students for the next stage of education or for employment or, perhaps, unemployment. These are ambitious targets which are often in conflict. The teacher is expected to be the social worker, the custodian and the quasi-parent as well as developing the pupil's capacity to learn. The ordering of priorities within this complex set of objectives is fraught with difficulties.

2. It is very difficult to *measure* whether or not objectives have been achieved in education. In commercial organizations it is possible to measure success in financial terms; sales have increased, profits are up, dividends are higher. Several factors militate against such straightforward evaluations in schools and colleges. Any assessment has to be long term to allow for the sheer length of the educational process – a minimum of eleven years for every citizen and several years more for an increasing proportion of young people. Even then certain aspects are not amenable to measurement. How do you assess the adequacy of socialization or the extent of personal development? It is possible to measure the results of public examinations and to test literacy and numeracy. Yet there is a danger that educational institutions will be assessed only in such terms while the more elusive criteria are undervalued or overlooked. As Handy (1984, p. 21) suggests, the absence of acceptable bases for evaluation creates serious management difficulties:

> Faced with blurred aims, conflicting functions and no simple way of measuring success, schools have a major management problem. Without clear and agreed objectives there are no criteria for deciding how to allocate resources – everything becomes a political debate about priorities. Without clear measures of success there are no obvious ways to assess the progress of individuals and departments – every judgement is subjective and personal.

3. The presence of *children* and young people as the focal points of educational institutions also contributes to this ambiguity. Pupils and students may be regarded as clients or outputs of schools and colleges. As clients there are unique characteristics which are explored below. As participants in a production process young people differ markedly from the raw material of industry and commerce. Children cannot be processed, programmed or manipulated. The learning process is built on personal relationships with all the idiosyncrasy and unpredictability that implies. This human element reinforces the problems of measurement discussed earlier.

4. The managers and teachers in schools (and to a lesser extent colleges) are from a common *professional* background with shared values, training and experience. As professionals, teachers claim a measure of autonomy in the classroom. The nature of the relationship with the class or group is not amenable to close definition or supervision. In addition, teachers as professionals should be able to participate in school or college decision-making because their commitment to the implementation of decisions is essential if the process is to be more than an empty ritual.

5. The *client* relationship between teacher and student differs in several respects from other professional–client links. Teachers have regular and extended contact with pupils; often several encounters a week for a period of years. Moreover, pupils have little opportunity to select their teachers. Children are required to spend at least eleven years as members of educational institutions and to accept that their teachers will be chosen for them. Glatter (1972, p. 8) emphasizes this unique aspect of educational institutions: 'This gives organisational problems in schools, and to only a slightly less degree in most other types of educational institution, . . . a fundamentally different character from those of nearly every other form of institution, even those which employ a high proportion of professional workers.'

6. There is a *fragmented* organization and management structure both within and impinging upon educational institutions. The climate for school and college decision-making is strongly influenced by a plethora of external agencies and groups. These include politicians, officials and inspectors at national level and, for some schools, equivalent groups in the locality, as well as parents and both formal and *ad hoc* pressure groups. There are also multiple decision points within schools and colleges and their subunits – departments, faculties, houses and years. This fragmentation makes it difficult to locate responsibility for management decision-making in schools and colleges.

7. Many senior and middle managers in schools, and to a lesser extent colleges, have *little time* for the managerial aspects of their work. In primary schools most or all staff are full-time class teachers. Only the head has significant opportunities to engage in managerial activity and in smaller schools the head is usually a class teacher. In secondary schools the head may be free of teaching commitments while deputies perhaps teach a 50 per cent timetable. Other staff have a heavy teaching load and managerial activities are squeezed into part of the remaining portion of 'directed time' or undertaken in the evenings or at weekends. The limited time available for management has significant implications for educational institutions. 'Teachers are teachers first and managers when they have to be, because managing is clearly a disruptive occupation if you have something else to do' (Handy and Aitken, 1986, p. 36).

## Educational management as an eclectic discipline

The debate about the validity of general management principles and exemplars for schools and colleges has been more muted in the 1990s. The growth and development of educational management as a distinct discipline has been accompanied by a more careful evaluation of the validity of material drawn from non-educational settings. Where ideas are drawn from industry, commerce or other parts of the public sector, they are generally adapted before being applied to education. Equally, it is unwise to ignore new developments simply because they do not emanate from the educational context:

There is great diversity in industry and commerce, and within this are to be found exemplary organizations and departments with whose managers most

teachers would find some rapport . . . [but] we readily acknowledge the cultural differences between schools and other organizations.
(Everard and Morris, 1990, pp. 10–12)

While rejecting the detailed application of management approaches from an industrial or commercial environment into schools, we should not fall into the belief that there is nothing to be learned from such experience.
(Osborne, 1990, p. 15)

The increasing interest in Total Quality Management (West-Burnham, 1992), human resource management (O'Neill, 1994) and marketing (Gray, 1991) in education are testimony to the view that ideas derived from general management can be successfully adapted for use in education. However, the special characteristics of schools and colleges imply caution in the application of management models or practices drawn from non-educational settings. As Baldridge *et al.* (1978, p. 9) recommend, careful evaluation and adaptation of such models is required before they can be applied with confidence to educational organizations.

> traditional management theories cannot be applied to educational institutions without carefully considering whether they will work well in that unique academic setting . . . We therefore must be extremely careful about attempts to manage or improve . . . education with 'modern management' techniques borrowed from business, for example. Such borrowing may make sense, but it must be approached very carefully.

## Managers and professionals

Schools and colleges are staffed predominantly by education professionals. This has implications for the nature of management in educational institutions because professionals seek a measure of control over their working environment. 'Schools are organisations of professionals who, in the manner of professionals, like to manage themselves' (Handy, 1984 p. 7).

Grace (1994, pp. 18–19) claims that professionalism was the dominant culture in English schools in the 1950s and 1960s:

> The discourse of modern management and bureaucracy was largely absent from schools. Headteachers were expected to relate to their colleagues within the principles and procedures of modern professionalism rather than managerialism . . . The empowerment of professional teachers and headteachers at this time empowered the culture of professionalism itself. The dominant notions of this era were that schools could be effectively organised and administered by a competent group of professionals. With the headteacher as leading professional and with a consultative mode of decision-making, a model form of internal school governance would be established.

The creation of large comprehensive schools modified this 'professional' model but it was the Education Reform Act that forced a different approach to the management of educational institutions. Principals and governors needed to develop new strategies for the management of the extra responsibilities imposed on schools and colleges. However, teachers' specialist qualifications and skills mean that they cannot be managed on a strictly hierarchical basis. 'The great weight of evidence is that the employment of large numbers of professionals in an organisation poses 'problems' for the application of the bureaucratic or hierarchical management model' (Osborne, 1990, p. 10).

## Leading professional or chief executive?

As we noted earlier (page 9), most teachers are usually too busy with their professional activities to be able to devote much of their time to management. Many management responsibilities are exercised on their behalf, often by heads and their senior management teams (Wallace and Hall, 1994). This may be acceptable to teachers as long as the managers are drawn from their own professional background. Most heads and principals are successful teachers or lecturers who have credibility within the profession and value their background as practitioners. In 1984, Hughes was able to claim that 'Heads . . . still regard themselves first and foremost as head *teachers*, not as managers or administrators' (Hughes, 1984, p. 4).

The management of professionals cannot be based simply on a bureaucratic structure but has to acknowledge the expertise of teachers as individuals, and as a group of staff within an institution. The integration of the needs of the organization and its clients with the expectations of the teachers is provided by heads and their senior teams, who are often sandwiched uncomfortably between the conflicting pressures of bureaucracy and professionalism. Hughes (1976) developed a 'professional as administrator' model which encompasses the head's dual role as the chief executive of a school and the leading professional within it. As chief executive, heads are accountable to external bodies for the successful management of the institution. As leading professional, they are responsible for the leadership of a group of teachers. Hughes (1976, p. 60) concludes that 'the professional as administrator fulfils his [*sic*] mediating role to a large extent by providing the kind of supervision of professional staff and the kind of organisational leadership in responding to external change, which is acceptable to professionals'.

The educational reforms of the late 1980s and 1990s have made it more difficult for heads and principals to sustain this dual role. In 1987, only 27.5 per cent of a sample of 500 secondary heads regarded themselves as 'leading professional and chief executive' while most of the rest preferred to emphasise their professional or 'senior teacher' role (Jones, 1987, p. 63). Subsequent research on secondary school heads in the East Midlands (Doughty, in preparation) and with primary school heads in a southern county (Cox, 1994) suggests that the 'chief executive' model has been accentuated since the Education Reform Act and that the 'leading professional' role is now ascribed to a deputy head.

Elliott and Hall (1994, p. 3) refer to 'the increasing business orientation of the British further education system', including the appointment of senior personnel from the business sector to the senior management teams of colleges. They express concern about the clash between business approaches and professional values:

The rift between managers and managed [has] deepened and the professional status and unique characteristics of teaching staff [is] unrecognised. The increasingly business orientations of the managers clash with the 'pedagogic' orientations of teaching staff, diverse though these are . . . There is little room in this transformation from service to business for dialogue about what constitutes quality learning in FE and the contribution of a 'quality' working environment for staff to achieving quality learning.

(Elliott and Hall, 1994, pp. 7–8)

Hellawell (1991) acknowledges the shift to the 'chief executive' model in primary education but believes that this can be avoided by increased use of delegation:

> Many heads and teachers are in broad agreement that primary school heads should preserve . . . their roles as 'leading professionals' and the overwhelming majority of heads are convinced at the same time that their 'chief executive' roles are becoming increasingly demanding . . . it is possible to delegate many of the functions of the chief executive role but it is impossible to delegate the key aspects of the leading professional role . . . it is self-evident that the head cannot lead by teaching example if s/he leaves the teaching to others.
>
> (Hellawell, 1991, p. 49)

Hughes, the originator of the model, argues that more flexible structures are required to enable educational leaders to sustain the professional aspects of their role despite the heightened managerial pressures:

> In a world of rapid and unpredictable change, it is increasingly clear that the senior educational administrator cannot be effective as a regulator, whose main concern is simply with maintaining the structure intact or adjusting the controls of the management cycle, while the . . . teachers get on with their tasks with a minimum of interaction with management or each other. A more creative and dynamic role is required, preferably in a collaborative framework, which includes involvement in defining and re-assessing goals, facilitating change, motivating staff and students, and external representation. Their professional background should enable the professionals-as-administrators . . . to retain credibility as 'leading professionals' while also being effective 'chief executives'.
>
> (Hughes, 1990, pp. 25–6)

Caldwell and Spinks (1992, pp. 49–50) advocate the adoption of transformational leadership in self-managing schools. This mode requires leaders to develop and communicate their vision of the school and to empower individuals and groups to make decisions in respect of their areas of responsibility. 'Transformational leaders succeed in gaining the commitment of followers to such a degree that those higher levels of accomplishment become virtually a moral imperative'. Empowering staff to make decisions is consistent with Hellawell's (1991) view that heads should delegate responsibilities in order to create time for their role as 'leading professionals'.

## Managing in a 'wild' environment

The climate of educational management in the 1990s is very different from that of the previous decade. When the first edition of this volume was prepared, the main issues were falling rolls, youth unemployment, spending cuts and low teacher morale. While these issues have not disappeared, and youth unemployment in particular has worsened, they have been supplemented by new problems which mean that educational institutions now provide an ever more searching test of managerial competence.

The Education Reform Act and subsequent legislation forced schools into the market place. The provision for open enrolment removed artificial limits on admissions and encouraged schools to compete for pupils. The income of schools is linked primarily to their success in recruiting pupils through the formula funding aspect of LMS. Unpopularity with parents leads to declining numbers with inevitable consequences for budgets, staffing levels and, ultimately, the survival of the institution. College income is also linked to their success in recruiting and retaining students (Coleman, Bush and Glover, 1994).

The shift from catchment areas to parental choice as the main determinant of school admissions graphically illustrates Carlson's (1975) distinction between 'wild' and 'domesticated' organizations. When schools had clearly delineated catchment areas they could be regarded as 'domestic' organizations, protected from their environment:

> There is no struggle for survival for this type of organization. Like the domesticated animal, these organizations are fed and cared for. Existence is guaranteed. Though their type of organization does compete in a restricted area for funds, funds are not closely tied to quality of performance. These organizations are domesticated in the sense that they are protected by the society they serve.
>
> (Carlson, 1975, p. 191)

The new emphasis on parental choice and formula funding means that schools now match Carlson's description of 'wild' organizations, which 'do struggle for survival. Their existence is not guaranteed, and they do cease to exist. Support for them is closely tied to quality of performance, and a steady flow of clients is not assured. Wild organizations are not protected at vulnerable points as are domesticated organizations' (Carlson, 1975, p. 191).

Colleges have long been required to compete in the market place but this is a relatively new phenomenon for schools which might have been regarded as 'domesticated' until the demographic and legislative changes of the 1980s. Now schools and colleges both exhibit many of the characteristics of 'wild' organizations, with their survival dependent on their ability to attract sufficient numbers of new clients.

The impact of environmental pressures on the nature and style of management will be discussed at length in subsequent chapters of this book but three major effects can be noted here:

1. The management of schools and colleges is dominated by *resource issues*. Heads and principals spend much of their time trying to ensure that their institutions attract sufficient pupils and students to be able to sustain their income and, therefore, current levels of staff and other real resources. Hoy and Miskel (1987) refer to the 'resource dependency' of schools and argue that leaders have to develop effective communication channels with those who control resources. Since the Education Reform Act, schools have become dependent on their reputation with parents, feeder schools and the community to recruit pupils and, hence, to obtain resources. Consequently, leaders have to invest time in nurturing these links in order to ensure the school's survival.

2.  The continuing uncertainty over levels of funding and the supply of clients may lead to an emphasis on decision-making for the *short-term*. Despite the increasing significance of development planning, schools as autonomous units may find it difficult to plan for the long-term because managers simply cannot assess staffing levels or the finance available for equipment or to support innovation. LMS means that staffing and curriculum may be subject to change according to the size of the next intake of pupils. For many managers there is limited value in planning beyond this point.
3.  The increasing vulnerability of schools and colleges to environmental pressures may lead to decision-making being *drawn to the centre* of many institutions. Teachers who have responsibility for relationships with governing bodies and the major external groups may be able to influence decisions by virtue of their control over these communication networks. Heads and principals often have the prime responsibility for links with the environment and their ability to interpret external pressures may serve to increase their power within the institution. The evidence from the GM sector in England and Wales is that autonomy has been accompanied by increased authority for heads, senior staff and a small group of active governors (Bush, Coleman and Glover, 1993; Thompson, 1992).

As environmental pressures intensify, managers require greater understanding, skill and resilience to sustain their institutions. Heads, principals and senior staff need an appreciation of the theory, as well as the practice, of educational management. Competence comprises an appreciation of concepts as well as a penchant for successful action. The next chapter examines the nature of theory in educational management and its contribution to good practice.

# References

Al-Khalifa, E. (1986) Can educational management learn from industry?, in E. Hoyle and A. McMahon (eds.) *World Yearbook of Education 1986: The Management of Schools*, Kogan Page, London.

Baldridge, J. V., Curtis, D. V., Ecker, G. and Riley, G. L. (1978) *Policy-Making and Effective Leadership*, Jossey Bass, San Francisco.

Barrell, G. (1982) Accountability in school management, *Education Today*, Vol. 32, no. 2, pp. 3–8. *Education Today* is the Journal of the College of Preceptors.

Bone, T. R. (1982) Educational administration, *British Journal of Educational Studies*, Vol. 30, no. 1, pp. 32–42.

Bush, T., Coleman, M. and Glover, D. (1993) *Managing Autonomous Schools: The Grant-Maintained Experience*, Paul Chapman Publishing, London.

Bush, T. and West-Burnham, J. (1994) Introduction: enduring principles in a climate of change in T. Bush and J. West-Burnham (eds.) *The Principles of Educational Management*, Longman, Harlow.

Caldwell, B. and Spinks, J. (1988) *The Self-Managing School*, The Falmer Press, London.

Caldwell, B and Spinks, J. (1992) *Leading the Self-Managing School*, The Falmer Press, London.

Carlson, R. O. (1975) Environmental constraints and organisational consequences: the public school and its clients, in J. V. Baldridge and T. E. Deal (eds.) *Managing Change in Educational Organisations*, McCutchan, Berkeley, © 1975 by McCutchan Publishing Corporation, Berkeley, CA.

Coleman, M., Bush, T. and Glover, D. (1994) *Managing Finance and External Relations*, Longman, Harlow.

Coulson, A. (1985) *The Managerial Behaviour of Primary School Heads*, Collected Original Resources in Education, Carfax Publishing Company, Abingdon.

Cox, S. (1994) Leading professional or chief executive: the changing role of the primary head teacher. Unpublished M.A. dissertation, University of Leicester.

Culbertson, J. (1980) Educational administration: where we are and where we are going presented at 4th International Intervisitation Program in Educational Administration, Vancouver.

Culbertson, J. (1983) Theory in educational administration: echoes from critical thinkers, *Educational Researcher*, Vol. 12, no. 10, pp. 15–22.

Cuthbert, R. (1984) *The Management Process*, E324 Management in Post Compulsory Education, Block 3, Part 2, Open University Press, Milton Keynes

Cyert, R. M. (1975) *The Management of Non Profit Organisations*, Lexington Books, Lexington, Massachusetts.

Doughty, J. (In preparation) The changing nature of secondary headship. Unpublished Ph.D thesis, University of Leicester.

Elliott, G. and Hall, V. (1994) FE Inc. – business orientation in further education and the introduction of human resource management, *School Organisation*, Vol. 14, no. 1, pp. 3–10.

Everard, K. B. and Morris, G. (1990) *Effective School Management*, Paul Chapman Publishing, London.

Fayol, H. (1916) *General and Industrial Management*, Pitman, London.

Glatter, R. (1972) *Management Development for the Education Profession*, Harrap, London, for the University of London Institute of Education.

Glatter, R. (1979) Educational policy and management: one field or two? *Educational Analysis*, Vol. 1, no. 2, pp. 15–24.

Grace, G. (1994) Headteachers in England: morality, professionalism and market relations, *American Educational Research Association*, April, New Orleans.

Gray, H. L. (1979) *The School as an Organisation*, Nafferton Books, Nafferton.

Gray, L. (1991) *Marketing Education*, Open University Press, Milton Keynes.

Haag, D. (1982) *The Right to Education: What Kind of Management?*, Unesco, Paris.

Handy, C. (1984) *Taken for Granted? Looking at Schools as Organisations*, Longman, York, for the Schools Council.

Handy, C. and Aitken, R. (1986) *Understanding Schools as Organizations*, Pelican, London.

Harries-Jenkins, G. (1984) State of the art review of the literature: education management part 1, *School Organisation and Management Abstracts*, Vol. 3, no. 4, pp. 213–33.

Hellawell, D. (1991) *Primary Headteacher Appraisal: A Research Study of the Attitudes of Headteachers*, Sheffield City Polytechnic, Sheffield.

Hoy, W. and Miskel, C. (1987) *Educational Administration: Theory, Research and Practice*, McGraw–Hill, New York.

Hoyle, E. (1981) *The Process of Management*, E323 Management and the School, Block 3, Part 1, Open University Press, Milton Keynes.

Hughes, M. G. (1976) The professional as administrator: the case of the secondary school head, in R. S. Peters (ed.) *The Role of the Head*, Routledge and Kegan Paul, London.

Hughes, M. G. (1984) Educational administration: pure or applied, *Studies in Educational Administration*, Vol. 35, pp. 1–10.

Hughes, M. (1985) Theory and practice in educational management, in M. Hughes, P. Ribbins and H. Thomas (eds.) *Managing Education: The System and the Institution*, Holt, Rinehart and Winston, London.

Hughes, M. (1990) Educational administration: international trends and issues, *International Journal of Educational Management*, Vol. 4, no. 1, pp. 22–30.

Hughes, M. and Bush, T. (1991) Theory and research as catalysts for change, in W. Walker, R. Farquhar and M. Hughes (eds.) *Advancing Education: School Leadership in Action*, The Falmer Press, London.

Hughes, M., Carter, J. and Fidler, B. (1981) *Professional Development Provision for Senior Staff in Schools and Colleges*, University of Birmingham, Birmingham.

Jones, A. (1987) *Leadership for Tomorrow's Schools*, Blackwell, Oxford.

Lofthouse, M. (1994) Managing the curriculum, in T. Bush and J. West-Burnham (eds.) *The Principles of Educational Management*, Longman, Harlow.

Maclure, S. (1988) *Education Reformed*, Hodder and Stoughton, Sevenoaks.

O'Neill, J. (1994) Managing human resources, in T. Bush and J. West-Burnham (eds.) *The Principles of Educational Management*, Longman, Harlow.

Osborne, A. (1990) The nature of education management, in B. Davies, L. Ellison, A. Osborne and J. West-Burnham (eds.) *Education Management for the 1990s*, Longman, Harlow.

School Management Task Force (1990) *Developing School Management: The Way Forward*, HMSO, London.

Squire, W. (1987) *Education Management in the UK*, Gower, Aldershot.

Taylor, F. W. (1947), *Principles of Scientific Management*, Harper and Row, New York.

Taylor, W. (1976) The head as manager: some criticisms, in R. S. Peters (ed.) *The Role of the Head*, Routledge and Kegan Paul, London.

Thompson, M. (1992) The experience of going grant-maintained: the perceptions of AMMA teacher representatives, *Journal of Teacher Development*, Vol. 1, no. 3, pp. 133–40.

Walker, W. G. (1984) Administrative narcissism and the tyranny of isolation: it decline and fall 1954–1984, *Educational Administration Quarterly*, Vol. 20, no. 4, pp. 6–23. Copyright © 1984 by W. G. Walker, reprinted by permission of Sag Publications, Inc.

Wallace, M. and Hall, V. (1994) *Inside the SMT*, London, Paul Chapman.

Weber, M. (1947) in T. Parsons (ed.) *The Theory Of Social and Economic Organ ization*, Free Press, Glencoe, Illinois and Collier-Macmillan, New York.

West-Burnham, J. (1992) *Managing Quality in Schools*, Longman, Harlow.

West-Burnham, J. (1994) Management in educational organizations, in T. Bush and J. West-Burnham (eds.) *The Principles of Educational Management*, Long man, Harlow.

# 2

# Models of Educational Management

## The theory/practice divide

Management is often regarded as essentially a practical activity. The determination of aims, the allocation of resources and the evaluation of effectiveness all involve action. Practitioners tend to be dismissive of theories and concepts for their alleged remoteness from the 'real' school situation. Dearden (1984, p. 4) claims that school and college staff have a somewhat ambivalent attitude towards theory. 'The teachers themselves commonly regard theory with a varying mixture of respect and suspicion: respect because it is thought of as difficult, and suspicion because its bearings are unclear on the detailed decision as to what to do next Monday morning.'

There is some evidence that the explicit and systematic use of theory as a guide to practice is unusual. Some commentators regard management as atheoretical. Willower (1980, p. 2), for example, asserts that 'the application of theories by practising administrators [is] a difficult and problematic undertaking. Indeed, it is clear that theories are simply not used very much in the realm of practice'. Holmes and Wynne (1989, pp. 1–2) are also sceptical about the value of theory in informing practice: 'There can be little genuine theory in educational administration. It is an applied field ultimately dependent on human will acting within a social context . . . So, it is unproductive to look for a set of theories . . . by which educational administrators may guide administrative behaviour.'

Hughes (1985, pp. 3 and 31) concedes that links between theory and practice have been weak: 'Theory and practice are uneasy, uncomfortable bedfellows, particularly when one is attempting to understand the complexities of human behaviour in organisational settings . . . It has been customary for practitioners to state the dichotomy in robust terms: airy-fairy theory versus down-to-earth practice.'

It is evident from these comments that theory and practice are often regarded as separate aspects of educational management. Academics develop and refine theory while managers engage in practice. In short, there is a theory/practice divide. Theory may be perceived as esoteric and remote from practice. Yet in an applied discipline such as educational management the acid test of theory is its relevance to practice. Theory is valuable and significant if it serves to explain practice and provide managers with a guide to action. The emphasis in this book is the use of theory to inform practice and to guide managers:

> Theories are most useful for influencing practice when they suggest new ways in which events and situations can be perceived. Fresh insight may be provided by focusing attention on possible interrelationships that the practitioner has failed to notice, and which can be further explored and tested through empirical research. If the result is a better understanding of practice, the theory-practice gap is significantly reduced for those concerned. Theory cannot then be dismissed as irrelevant.
>
> (Hughes and Bush, 1991, p. 234).

## The relevance of theory to good practice

If practitioners shun theory then they must rely on experience as a guide to action. In deciding on their response to a problem they draw on a range of options suggested by previous experience with that type of issue. Teachers sometimes explain their decisions as just 'common sense'. However, such apparently pragmatic decisions are often based on implicit theories: 'Common-sense knowledge . . . inevitably carries with it unspoken assumptions and unrecognised limitations. Theorising is taking place without it being acknowledged as such' (Hughes, 1985, p. 31). When a teacher or a manager takes a decision it reflects in part that person's view of the organization. Such views or preconceptions are coloured by experience and by the attitudes engendered by that experience. These attitudes take on the character of frames of reference or theories which inevitably influence the decision-making process.

The use of the term 'theory' need not imply something remote from the day-to-day experience of the teacher. Rather, theories and concepts can provide a framework for managerial decisions. 'There is nothing more practical than a good theory. . . . It can . . . help the practitioner to unify and focus his [*sic*] views on an organisation, on his role and relationships within the organisation, and on the elusive phenomena of leadership and achievement' (Landers and Myers, 1977, p. 365). Theory serves to provide a rationale for decision-making. Managerial activity is enhanced by an explicit awareness of the theoretical framework underpinning practice in educational institutions. As a result some academics and practitioners 'now vigorously challenge the traditional view that practical on the job experience *on its own* provides adequate management training in education' (Hughes, 1984, p. 5).

There are four main arguments to support the view that managers have much to learn from an appreciation of theory.

1. Reliance on facts as the sole guide to action is unsatisfactory because all evidence requires *interpretation*. Life in schools and colleges is too complex to enable practitioners to make decisions simply on an event by event basis. A frame of reference is needed to provide the insight for this important management task. As Bolman and Deal (1984, p. 16) suggest, 'We have to develop patterns and frames in order to make sense of the complexities of everyday life'.

2. Dependence on personal *experience* in interpreting facts and making decisions is narrow because it discards the knowledge of others. Familiarity with the arguments and insights of theorists enables the practitioner to deploy a wide range of experience and understanding in resolving the problems of today. Walker (1984, p. 18) makes a convincing case for practitioner awareness of theory:

> As a result of the new horizons that have been opened up, scholars and practitioners alike have a much richer platform of ideas on which to base their diagnosis and to take action. A well prepared administrator can hardly avoid knowing that there is available to him or her a wide and challenging literature that promises useful alternatives for action.

3. Errors of *judgement* can occur while experience is being acquired. Mistakes are costly in both human and material terms. Resources are limited but the needs of children and students are even more important. 'In education we just cannot throw away the flawed product as waste and start again' (Hughes, 1984, p. 5).

4. Experience may be particularly unhelpful as the sole guide to action when the practitioner begins to operate in a different *context*. Organizational variables may mean that practice in one school or college has little relevance in the new environment. A broader awareness of theory and practice may be valuable as the manager attempts to interpret behaviour in the fresh situation.

Of course, theory is useful only so long as it has relevance to practice in education. The practitioner and the scholar have different purposes in gaining an appreciation of theory, as Theodossin (1982, p. 137) makes clear: 'The academic tends to want understanding for knowledge, while the manager seeks understanding for action: to enable him to perceive the possible options open to him and the likely consequences of each.' The relevance of theory for the manager in education should be judged by the extent to which it informs managerial action and contributes to the resolution of practical problems inside schools and colleges.

## The nature of theory in educational management

There is no single all-embracing theory of educational management. In part this reflects the astonishing diversity of educational institutions, ranging from small rural primary schools to very large universities and colleges. It relates also to the varied nature of the problems encountered in schools and colleges which require different approaches and solutions. Above all, it reflects the multifaceted nature of theory in education and the social sciences: 'Students of educational management who turn to organisational theory for guidance in their attempt to understand and manage educational institutions will not find a single, universally-applicable theory but a multiplicity of theoretical approaches each jealously guarded by a particular epistemic community' (Ribbins, 1985, p. 223).

House (1981) argues that theories or 'perspectives' in education are not the same as scientific theories. The latter comprises a set of beliefs, values and techniques that are shared within a particular field of enquiry. The dominant theory eventually comes under challenge by the emergence of new facts which the theory cannot explain. Subsequently a new theory is postulated which does explain these new facts. However, the physical world itself remains constant.

Theories of education and the social sciences are very different from scientific theories. These perspectives relate to a changing situation and comprise different ways of seeing a problem rather than a scientific consensus as to what is true. House (1981, p. 17) suggests that, in this sense, the perspective is a weaker claim to knowledge than a scientific theory. In education several perspectives may be valid simultaneously:

> Our understanding of knowledge utilisation processes is conceived not so much as a set of facts, findings, or generalisations but rather as distinct perspectives which combine facts, values and presuppositions into a complex screen through which knowledge utilisation is seen. . . . Through a particular screen one sees certain events, but one may see different scenes through a different screen.

The models discussed in this book should be regarded as alternative ways of portraying events, as House suggests, rather than the absolute truths of scientific theory. In choosing one perspective the teacher tends to exclude the other ways of understanding events: 'All perspectives offer insights in exchange for limitations in approach' (Silverman, 1970, p. 44).

The existence of several different perspectives creates what Bolman and Deal (1984) describe as 'conceptual pluralism'. Each theory has something to offer in explaining behaviour and events in educational institutions. The perspectives favoured by managers, explicitly or implicitly, inevitably influence or determine decision-making. Bolman and Deal (1984, p. 4) argue that perspectives or 'frames' form the basis for managerial practice: 'Frames are windows on the world. Frames filter out some things while allowing others to pass through easily. Frames help us to order the world and decide what action to take.'

Morgan (1986) discusses the concept of organizational culture and emphasizes the diversity of theories of management and organization. He uses 'metaphors' to explain 'the complex and paradoxical character of organisational life' (Morgan, 1986, p. 13). He describes theory in similar terms to House (1981):

> Theories and explanations of organisational life are based on metaphors that lead us to see and understand organisations in distinctive yet partial ways . . . the use of metaphor implies *a way of thinking* and *a way of seeing* that pervades how we understand our world . . . metaphor . . . always produces this kind of one-sided insight. In highlighting certain interpretations it tends to force others into a background role.
>
> (Morgan, 1986, pp. 12–13)

One of the confusing aspects of educational management theory is the use of different terms to explain similar phenomena. While House (1981) prefers 'perspective', Bolman and Deal (1984) choose 'frame' and Morgan (1986) opts for 'metaphor'. Boyd (1992, p. 506) adds to the confusion by referring to 'paradigms', a term he admits to using 'loosely': 'By paradigm is meant a model or theory; with models or theories often guiding, consciously or sub consciously, our thinking about such things as organizations, leadership and policy.' These terms are broadly similar and reflect the preferences of the authors rather than any significant differences in meaning. They will be used interchangeably in this text.

Theories of educational management are endowed with different terminology but they all emanate from organization theory or management theory. The former tends to be theory for understanding while management theory has more direct relevance for practice. Hoyle (1986, pp. 1 and 20) distinguishes between these two broad approaches:

> Organisation theory is theory-for-understanding. We can thus make a broad distinction between organisation theory and management theory, which is practical theory and hence has a narrower focus. However, the distinction cannot be pressed too hard since management theory is grounded in, and the research which it generates contributes to, organisation theory . . . the case for organisation theory is that it enhances our understanding of the management component and . . . that it provides a loose organising framework for a variety of studies of schools.

Holmes and Wynne (1989, p. 29) take a much more critical view of the value of organization theory for educational management: 'Unfortunately, there is no empirically proven theory of school organization so such texts [of school administration] are reduced to describing scattered pieces of research held together with inconclusive argument.' This assessment is much too pessimistic and greatly undervalues the theory development and related empirical research on aspects of schools and colleges as organizations.

The models discussed in this book are broad compilations of the main theories of educational management and are largely based on organization theory. However, by applying theory to practice throughout the text, management theories are developed and tested for their applicability to schools and colleges and to individual managers within them.

## The characteristics of educational management theory

Most theories of educational management possess three major characteristics:

1. Theories tend to be *normative* in that they reflect beliefs about the nature of educational institutions and the behaviour of individuals within them. To a greater or lesser extent, theorists express views about how schools and colleges should be managed rather than simply describing aspects of management or explaining the organizational structure of the school or college. When, for example, practitioners or academics claim that decisions in schools are reached following a participative process they may be expressing normative judgements rather than analysing actual practice.

2. Theories tend to be *selective* or partial in that they emphasize certain aspects of the institution at the expense of other elements. The espousal of one theoretical model leads to the neglect of other approaches. Schools and colleges are arguably too complex to be capable of analysis through a single dimension. An explanation of educational institutions using a political perspective, for example, may focus on the formation of interest groups and

on the bargaining between groups and individuals. This approach offers valuable insights, as we shall see in Chapter 5, but this emphasis necessarily means that other valid theories of school and college management may be underestimated. A few writers (Enderud, 1980; Davies and Morgan, 1983; Ellstrom, 1983;) have presented syntheses of different approaches in an attempt to achieve an overall approach to organizations but with only limited success.

3.  Theories of educational management are often based on, or supported by, *observation* of practice in educational institutions. Walker (1978, p. 100) asserts that theories require the support of regular and methodical observation: 'A crucial aspect of good theory development . . . relates to the area of systematic and repeated observation. Thus while it is possible to explain or predict a behaviour on the evidence of a single observation the prediction is very much more powerful if it is systematically and repeatedly observed.' While many theories of educational management are based on observation, advocates of the subjective model are sceptical of this stance. As we shall see in Chapter 6, subjective theorists prefer to emphasize the perceptions and interpretations of individuals within organizations. In this view observation is suspect because it does not reveal the meanings placed on events by participants.

    Those perspectives which are based on data from systematic observation are sometimes called 'grounded theory'. Because such approaches are derived from empirical inquiry in schools and colleges, they are more likely to be perceived as relevant by practitioners. As Glaser and Strauss (1967, p. 3) aptly claim, 'generating grounded theory is a way of arriving at theory suited to its supposed uses'.

Theory in educational management thus tends to be normative, selective and often based on observation in educational settings. These qualities overlap and interpenetrate, as Theodossin (1983, p. 89) demonstrates: 'Inevitably . . . research involves selection; selection is determined by, and determines, perspective; perspective limits vision; vision generates questions; and questions in turn help to shape and influence the answers.'

## Gender and educational management

Women are greatly underrepresented in senior posts in education as in many other occupations. In secondary schools in 1991, 48 per cent of all teachers but only 21 per cent of the headteachers, were women (Coleman, 1994b). There are many possible reasons for this disparity but there can be little doubt that women are disadvantaged and that this represents an enormous waste of human capital.

Among the reasons advanced for the low proportion of women in senior posts is the alleged 'male' image of management which may be unappealing to women. This model includes 'aggressive competitive behaviours, an emphasis on control rather than negotiation and collaboration, and the pursuit of competition rather than shared problem-solving' (Al-Khalifa 1992, p. 100). The male domination, or 'androcentricity', of educational management is evident in the United States where school administration evolved into a largely male profession disconnected from the mainly female occupation of teaching. Boyd (1992, p. 509) implies that this led to discrimination in the allocation of administrative posts: 'The abilities and values of women were passed over, as careers in school administration were more driven by male sponsorship than by merit and open competition . . . school administration became far more concerned with hierarchy, control and efficiency than with issues of curriculum, pedagogy, and educational values.'

The androcentricity of educational management has led certain writers (Shakeshaft, 1987; Ozga, 1993) to claim that theory has failed to acknowledge the different values of women and remains largely rooted in a male perspective. The difficulty is that there is little clarity about what constitutes a distinctive female theory of educational management. Hall (1993, pp. 43–4) concludes that

There is relatively little to date in research about women managers that can be used to challenge theories of educational management or lead to their reconceptualisation to include both women and men . . . Research is needed that challenges traditional stereotypes of what constitutes appropriate management behaviour and process. The association of management and masculinity has not been established as a fact yet it is treated as such, with negative consequences for women in education . . . theory and prescriptions for action [would be] transformed by the inclusion of gender as a relevant concept for understanding educational management.

Wallace and Hall's (1994, p. 39) research on senior management teams in secondary schools suggests that it is possible for management to incorporate both female and male styles: 'The decision to adopt a team approach seems to signify a shift in leadership style towards an "androgynous" model which posits the possibility for leaders to exhibit the wide range of qualities which are present in both men and women.' Gray (1989) adopts a similar approach in distinguishing between 'feminine' and 'masculine' paradigms in school management. Feminine characteristics include 'caring', 'creative' and 'intuitive' dimensions while the masculine paradigm features 'competitive', 'highly regulated' and 'disciplined' elements. Individual managers may possess qualities from both paradigms regardless of their gender.

A number of the six models presented in this book have been aligned with 'male' or 'female' qualities. The gender implications of the theories will be discussed at appropriate points in the text.

## Models of educational management – an introduction

Many different theories of educational management have been presented by various writers. These perspectives overlap in several respects. A further complication is that similar models are given different names or, in certain cases, the same term is used to denote different approaches. A degree of integration of these theories is required so that they can be presented in a clear and discrete manner. Cuthbert (1984, p. 39) explains why there is a lack of clarity:

The study of management in education is an eclectic pursuit. Models have been borrowed from a wide range of disciplines, and in a few cases developed specifically to explain unique features of educational institutions.

To comprehend the variety of models available we need some labels and categories that allow us to consider different ideas in a sensible order.

The approach to theory adopted in this book has certain similarities with Cuthbert's (1984) presentation of models in five distinct groups. Cuthbert's categories are analytic-rational, pragmatic-rational, political, models that stress ambiguity, and phenomenological and interactionist models. The latter three groups are the same as three of the models discussed in this text although I prefer the term subjective rather than phenomenological or interactionist. Cuthbert compares his models in the following terms:

a) the level of agreement among people in the organization about the objectives of their joint efforts;
b) different ideas about the way in which performance can and should be evaluated;
c) different ideas about the concept and the meaning of organization structure.

Two of the criteria used by Cuthbert are similar to two of the four main elements used in this text to distinguish between the models.

Several writers have chosen to present theories in distinct groups or bundles but they differ in the models chosen, the emphasis given to particular approaches and the terminology used to describe them:

- Bolman and Deal (1984); three 'common sense perspectives' – personalistic, rational and power.
- Ellstrom (1983); four organizational models – rational, political, social system and anarchistic.
- Sergiovanni (1984); four perspectives – efficiency, the person, politics and the cultural view.

In this book the main theories are classified into six major models of educational management. While this division differs somewhat from the categorization of other writers, these models are given significant attention in the literature of educational management and have been subject to a degree of empirical verification in British education. The six theories are illustrated extensively by examples of practice drawn from primary schools, secondary schools and colleges.

The models vary in the extent of their applicability to the different types of institution and, to a lesser degree, *within* any one section of education. The six models are:

1. formal
2. collegial
3. political
4. subjective
5. ambiguity
6. cultural.

In the first edition of this book only five models were identified. A chapter on the cultural model has been added to this version because of the increasing significance of this approach in the literature and because some empirical work has now been undertaken in British schools and elsewhere in the English speaking world.

## Analysing the models

The analysis of these six models includes consideration of four main elements which are valuable in distinguishing the theories. These criteria are as follows:

1. The level of agreement about the *goals* or objectives of the institution. There is increasing emphasis on goals in the literature on school improvement. Blum and Butler (1989, p. 19) stress the need for clear objectives if schools are to be effective:

   > School leaders must set an overall direction for the improvement of the school within relevant national and local policies. They must define the school's 'mission' or propose for it an educational 'vision' . . . Closely associated with the vision is the identification of short-term, manageable goals which are in line with the overall direction of the school.

   The theories differ in that some emphasize organizational aims while others focus on individual purposes. Certain models feature agreement about objectives but others stress conflict over aims or point to difficulties in defining purpose within educational organizations.
2. The meaning and validity of organizational *structures* within educational institutions. Hoyle (1986) refers to the twin dimensions of people and structure. An emphasis on structure leads to the notion of individuals being defined by their roles while a focus on people leads to the predominance of personality in determining behaviour.

   According to some theorists, structure is an objective fact while others believe that it is the subjective creation of individuals within the institution. Another group argues that structure is a matter for negotiation or dispute while others claim that the structure is one of the many ambiguous features of schools and colleges.
3. The relationship between the institution and its external *environment*. The shift to self-managing schools and colleges, discussed in Chapter 1, increases the significance of the relationships that staff and governors must have with a wide range of external groups and individuals. The need to satisfy current and potential clients, and to maintain a good reputation in the community, has been heightened by the close relationship between recruitment and funding levels (Coleman, Bush and Glover, 1994).

   The nature of these external relationships is a key element in the differences between models: 'Any theory of organisations must specify the nature of their relationships with the wider society' (Silverman, 1970, p. 23). Some writers regard the head or principal as the sole or major contact with the outside world while others suggest a wider range of contacts. Links may be regarded as essentially co-operative in nature or they may be thought of as political, with conflict between the institution and external agencies. Other approaches emphasize the ambiguity of such relationships.

4. The most appropriate *leadership* strategies for educational institutions. Coleman (1994a) stresses the centrality of leadership in organizations. Analysts have different views about the nature of educational leadership according to the theories they espouse. Some assume that heads take the lead in establishing objectives and in decision-making while others regard the head as one figure within a participative system. Certain approaches stress conflict inside institutions and emphasize the head's role as negotiator while others point to the limitations of an active leadership role within essentially ambiguous institutions.

These criteria serve to emphasize the great differences in approach between the various models and reinforce the view that theories are normative and selective. Mangham (1979, pp. x–xi) argues that

> Each of us approaches events and circumstances with bundles of values and related assumptions which constitute our basic frames of reference or conceptual models in terms of which we analyse and comment upon that with which we find ourselves confronted. Like it or not we do not see a *real* world that is truly there; each of us *interprets* his [*sic*] environment and copes with it by fitting it into meaningful patterns.

In subsequent chapters of this book we examine these different interpretations of the nature of organization and management in schools and colleges.

# References

Al-Khalifa, E. (1992) Management by halves: women teachers and school management, in N. Bennett, M. Crawford and C. Riches (eds.) *Managing Change in Education: Individual and Organizational Perspectives*, Paul Chapman Publishing, London.

Blum, R. E. and Butler, J. A. (1989) The role of school leaders in school improvement, in R. E. Blum and J. A. Butler (eds.) *School Leader Development for School Improvement*, Acco, Leuven, Belgium.

Bolman, L. G. and Deal, T. E. (1984) *Modern Approaches to Understanding and Managing Organisations*, Jossey Bass, San Francisco.

Boyd, W. (1992) The power of paradigms: reconceptualizing educational policy and management, *Educational Administration Quarterly*, Vol. 28, no. 4, pp. 504–28, November.

Coleman, M. (1994a) Leadership in educational management, in T. Bush and J. West-Burnham (eds.) *The Principles of Educational Management*, Longman, Harlow.

Coleman, M. (1994b) Women in educational management in T. Bush and J. West-Burnham (eds.) *The Principles of Educational Management*, Longman, Harlow.

Coleman, M., Bush, T. and Glover, D. (1994) *Managing Finance and External Relations*, Longman, Harlow.

Cuthbert, R (1984) *The Management Process, E324 Management in Post Compulsory Education, Block 3, Part 2*, Open University Press, Milton Keynes.

Davies, J. L. and Morgan, A. W. (1983) Management of higher education in a period of contraction and uncertainty, in O. Boyd-Barrett, T. Bush, J. Goodey, I. McNay and M. Preedy (eds.) *Approaches to Post School Management*, Paul Chapman, London.

Dearden, R. F. (1984) *Theory and Practice in Education*, Routledge and Kegan Paul, London.

Ellstrom, P. E. (1983) Four faces of educational organisations, *Higher Education*, Vol. 12, pp. 231–41.

Enderud, H. (1980) Administrative leadership in organised anarchies, *International Journal of Institutional Management in Higher Education*, Vol. 4, no. 3, pp. 235–53.

Glaser, B. G. and Strauss, A. L. (1967) *The Discovery of Grounded Theory*, Weidenfeld and Nicolson, London.

Gray, H. (1989) Gender considerations in school management: masculine and feminine leadership styles, in C. Riches and C. Morgan (eds.) *Human Resource Management in Education*, Open University Press, Milton Keynes.

Hall, V. (1993) Women in educational management: a review of research in Britain, in J. Ouston (ed.) *Women in Educational Management*, Longman, Harlow.

Holmes, M. and Wynne, E. (1989) *Making the School an Effective Community: Belief, Practice and Theory in School Administration*, The Falmer Press, Lewes.

House, E. R. (1981) Three perspectives on innovation, in R. Lehming and M. Kane (eds.) *Improving Schools: Using What We Know*, Sage Publications, Beverly Hills.

Hoyle, E. (1986) *The Politics of School Management*, Hodder and Stoughton, Sevenoaks.

Hughes, M. G. (1984) Educational administration; pure or applied, *Studies in Educational Administration*, Vol. 35, pp. 1–10.

Hughes, M. (1985) Theory and practice in educational management, in M. Hughes, P. Ribbins and H. Thomas (eds.) *Managing Education: The System and the Institution*, Holt, Rinehart and Winston, London.

Hughes, M. and Bush, T. (1991) Theory and research as catalysts for change, in W. Walker, R. Farquhar and M. Hughes (eds.) *Advancing Education: School Leadership in Action*, The Falmer Press, London.

Landers, T. J. and Myers, J. G. (1977) *Essentials Of School Management*, W. B. Saunders, Philadelphia.

Mangham, I. (1979) *The Politics of Organisational Change*, Associated Business Press, Ludgate House, Fleet Street, London.

Morgan, G. (1986) *Images of Organization*, Sage, Newbury Park, California.

Ozga, J. (1993) *Women in Educational Management*, Open University Press, Milton Keynes.

Ribbins, P. (1985) Organisation theory and the study of educational institutions, in M. Hughes, P. Ribbins and H. Thomas (eds.) *Managing Education: The System and the Institution*, Holt, Rinehart and Winston, London.

Sergiovanni, T. J. (1984) Cultural and competing perspectives in administrative theory and practice, in T. J. Sergiovanni and J. E. Corbally, *Leadership and Organisational Culture*, University of Illinois Press, Chicago.

Shakeshaft, C. (1987) *Women in Educational Administration*, Sage, Newbury Park, California.

Silverman, D. (1970) *The Theory of Organisations*, Gower, Aldershot.

Theodossin, E. (1982) Managing education and management theory, *Coombe Lodge Reports*, Vol. 15, no. 4, pp. 137–48.

Theodossin, E. (1983) Theoretical perspectives on the management of planned educational change, *British Education Research Journal*, Vol. 9, no. 1, pp. 81–90.

Walker, W. G. (1978) Values, unorthodoxy and the 'unscientific' in educational administration research, *Educational Administration*, Vol. 6, no. 2, pp. 94–106.

Walker, W. G. (1984) Administrative narcissism and the tyranny of isolation: its decline and fall, 1954–1984, *Educational Administration Quarterly*, Vol. 20, no. 4, pp. 6–23. Copyright © 1984 W. G. Walker. Reprinted by permission of Sage Publications, Inc.

Wallace, M. and Hall, V. (1994) *Inside the SMT: Teamwork in Secondary School Management*, Paul Chapman Publishing, London.

Willower, D. J. (1980) Contemporary issues in theory in educational administration, *Educational Administration Quarterly*, Vol. 16, no. 3, pp. 1–25. Copyright © 1980 D. J. Willower. Reprinted by permission of Sage Publications, Inc.

# 3

# Formal Models

## Central features of formal models

Formal model is an umbrella term used to embrace a number of similar but not identical approaches. The title 'formal' is used because these theories emphasize the official and structural elements of organizations. There is a focus on pursuing institutional objectives through rational approaches. The definition suggested below incorporates the main features of these perspectives:

Formal models assume that organizations are hierarchical systems in which managers use rational means to pursue agreed goals. Heads possess authority legitimized by their formal positions within the organization and are accountable to sponsoring bodies for the activities of their institutions.

The various formal models have several common features:

1. They tend to treat organizations as *systems*. According to Moran (1972, p. 3) 'a system . . . consists of a set of interacting parts and exhibits some kind of integrity as a whole'. This emphasis on interdependence implies that subunits such as departments or pastoral units are systemically related to each other and to the institution itself.
2. Formal models give prominence to the *official structure* of the organization. Formal structures are often represented by organization charts which show the authorized pattern of relationships between members of the institution. Structural models do not adequately reflect the many informal contacts within schools and colleges but they do help to represent the more stable and official aspects of organizations.
3. In formal models the official structures of the organization tend to be *hierarchical*. Organization charts emphasize vertical relationships between staff. In secondary schools and colleges staff are responsible to heads of department who, in turn, are answerable to heads and principals for the activities of their departments. The hierarchy thus represents a means of control for leaders over their staff. 'Most schools remain static, hierarchical and paternalistic in character. Internally they retain a tight authority structure' (Renshaw, 1974, p. 9).

4. All formal approaches typify schools and colleges as *goal-seeking* organizations. The institution is thought to have official purposes which are accepted and pursued by members of the organization. Livingstone (1974, p. 20), for example, claims that organizations and objectives are inevitably intertwined: 'Every organisation . . . has a goal towards which it strives . . . Having a purpose is inherent in the notion of organisation.' Because schools and colleges are regarded as hierarchical organizations it is assumed that heads and principals take the leading role in determining the goals of their institutions: 'Successful heads are *goal-orientated* insofar as they have a vision of how they would like to see their schools develop' (Coulson, 1985, p. 65).

5. Formal models assume that managerial decisions are made through a *rational* process. Typically, all the options are considered and evaluated in terms of the goals of the organization. The most suitable alternative is then selected to enable those objectives to be pursued. The essence of this approach is that decision-making is thought to be an objective, detached and intellectual process. Advocates of the rational model 'see the managerial elite as using rational and logical means to pursue clear and discrete ends set forth in official statements of goals' (Perrow, 1961, p. 88).

6. Formal approaches present the *authority* of leaders as essentially a product of their official positions within the organization. Heads and principals possess authority over other staff because of their formal roles within schools and colleges. Their power is regarded as positional: 'Members work under accepted leaders exercising legitimate authority . . . by virtue of office held at a particular time' (Ferguson, 1980, p. 535).

7. In formal models there is an emphasis on the *accountability* of the organization to its sponsoring body. Most schools remain responsible to the local education authority (LEA). Colleges and GM schools are accountable to their funding bodies, the Further Education Funding Council (FEFC) and the Funding Agency for Schools (FAS). In the climate of self-management generated by the Education Reform Act, heads and principals are answerable to their governing bodies which have enhanced responsibility for finance and staff management.

These seven basic features are present to a greater or lesser degree in each of the individual theories which together comprise the formal models. These are:

- structural models;
- systems models;
- bureaucratic models;
- rational models;
- hierarchical models.

These different theories overlap significantly and the main elements are often very similar despite their different titles. There are variations in emphasis but the central components appear in most of the individual theories.

## Structural models

Structural models stress the primacy of organizational structure but the key elements are compatible with the central features of any formal model. Consider this passage from Bolman and Deal (1984, pp. 31–2):

The structural perspective is based on a set of core assumptions:

1. Organizations exist primarily to accomplish established goals.
2. For any organization, there is a structure appropriate to the goals, the environment, the technology, and the participants.
3. Organizations work most effectively when environmental turbulence and the personal preferences of participants are constrained by norms of rationality.
4. Specialization permits higher levels of individual expertise and performance.
5. Coordination and control are accomplished best through the exercise of authority and impersonal rules.
6. Structures can be systematically designed and implemented.
7. Organizational problems usually reflect an inappropriate structure and can be resolved through redesign and reorganization.

Structuralists tend to see organizations as relatively closed systems pursuing fairly explicit goals. Under those conditions, organizations can operate rationally with high degrees of certainty and predictability. If organizations are highly dependent on the environment, they are continually vulnerable to environmental influence or interference. To reduce their vulnerability, a variety of structural mechanisms are created to protect central activities from fluctuation and uncertainty.

The structural assumptions identified by Bolman and Deal, including the goal orientation, the rationality, the exercise of authority and the reference to systems, are consistent with the central features of formal models discussed earlier. The categorization of organizations as relatively closed systems is not shared by some of the other approaches. Some theorists regard educational institutions as 'open systems', as we shall see in the next section. However, the ability of schools and colleges to respond to their environments may depend on the responsiveness of their organizational structure (Clark, 1983).

Becher and Kogan (1992) propose a structural model which has four levels. These are as follows:

1. The *Central Level*, including the various national and local authorities who are between them charged with overall planning, resource allocation and the monitoring of standards.
2. The *Institution* as defined in law and convention. This includes all schools and colleges.
3. The *Basic Unit* which corresponds with departments or faculties in colleges and with departments and pastoral units in schools.
4. The *Individual* level comprises teachers, students or pupils and support staff, but Becher and Kogan focus mainly on teachers because 'it is they who normally play the main role in shaping academic and curricular policy' (Becher and Kogan 1992, p. 9).

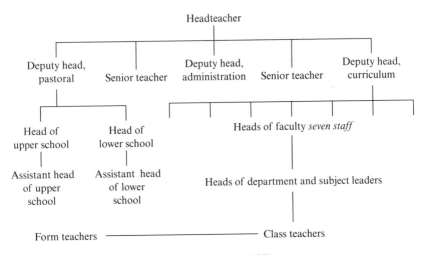

**Figure 3.1**   The Pensnett School structure (1986/87)

This structural model features normative and operational modes. The normative mode relates to the monitoring and maintenance of values within the system as a whole. The operational mode refers to the business of carrying out practical tasks at different levels within the system.

Relationships between levels can be categorized as either normative or operational. Normative relationships involve appraisal or judgement while operational relationships relate to the allocation of resources, responsibilities and tasks.

Becher and Kogan leave open the nature of the relationships between their four levels. Their structural model does not assume hierarchical relationships. However, school and college structures are usually portrayed as vertical and hierarchical. The structure of Pensnett comprehensive school, Dudley, in 1986–7, for example, appeared to be hierarchical (see Figure 3.1).

The Pensnett structure at that time distinguished between academic and pastoral activities, leading to an academic/pastoral 'divide' widely acknowledged by the staff: 'There is a definite split. The academic/pastoral divide is unfortunate. There are two separate empires; two compartments with a partition. Backbiting exists between faculty heads and pastoral staff' (Teacher quoted by Bush, 1989, p. 5). The structure shown in Figure 3.1 was modified by 1988 but this example illustrates the point that structures may facilitate or inhibit effective management and good relationships in schools and colleges.

College structures have traditionally been hierarchical (Brannen, Holloway and Peeke, 1981). However, many colleges have adopted new structures during the 1980s and 1990s. A Further Education Staff College survey (1989) shows that 40 per cent of colleges had modified or replaced their departmental structures during the previous eight years or were currently reviewing their structures. Despite these changes, 79 per cent of colleges still retained a departmental or faculty structure.

Structures are not inevitably hierarchical. Those which are apparently hierarchical may be used to facilitate delegation and participation in decision-making. This may occur where budgets are delegated to departments.

In many primary schools flatter structures are in evidence, often with a team approach to curricular issues. The head of Wroxham school in Potters Bar, Hertfordshire, may be typical in avoiding subunits: 'I don't see the school as two departments so I would not want a head of infants or a head of juniors. I prefer a whole school approach' (Bush, 1988, p. 29).

## The resilience of structure

It is easy to dismiss organizational structures as a rigid, over-formal presentation of relationships in educational institutions. All schools and colleges benefit from informal contacts not represented on organization charts. In addition, formal structures conceal a range of different styles of management. Yet structures remain powerful influences on the nature and direction of development within institutions, as Clark (1983, p. 114) makes clear:

> Academic structures do not simply move aside or let go: what is in place heavily conditions what will be. The heavy hand of history is felt in the structures and beliefs that development has set in place. As systems grow larger and more complex, their internal structures acquire greater momentum, thrusting themselves powerfully into the future and snapping back with considerable resilience after imposed changes seemingly altered their ways. . . . We do not begin to know the score in the study of academic change until we understand how current structures stack the deck.

## Systems models

Systems theories emphasize the unity and integrity of the organization and focus on the interaction between its component parts, and with the external environment. Their advocates tend to be evangelical in pressing the merits of such models: 'Quality control and maximum effectiveness in a large educational organisation are possible only by use of the systems approach. This type of management is imperative in larger systems; it is also the key to producing better results in small school systems' (Landers and Myers, 1977, p. 416).

Systems models stress the unity and *coherence* of the organization. Schools and colleges are thought to have integrity as prime institutions. Members of the organization, and those external to it, recognize the school or college as a meaningful entity. Staff and students may feel that they 'belong' to the place where they teach or learn. However, there are dangers in too great an emphasis on the organization rather than the people within it, as Silverman (1970, p. 29) points out: 'Systems theorists believe that it is useful to follow the common-sense practice of attributing actions to organisations themselves as well as to the members of organisations . . . however, one runs the risk of attributing human characteristics to social constructs.' Greenfield (1973; 1975) has been the most persistent critic of this tendency to reify organizations as we shall see in Chapter 6.

Systems approaches share with other formal models the emphasis on agreed organizational *objectives*. It is assumed that the total system has objectives which have the support of its members. The institution is thought to develop policies in pursuit of these objectives and to assess the effectiveness of such policies. Systems theories play down or ignore the possibility that goals may be contested or that individuals may have purposes independent of the formal aims of the organization.

Systems models emphasize the concept of a system *boundary*. The boundary is an essential element in the definition of the system, distinguishing the organization and its members from the external environment. 'Drawing a boundary not only defines the extent of the system, it also defines that system's environment' (Latcham and Cuthbert, 1983, p. 190).

## Closed or open systems

Systems theories are usually categorized as either *closed* or *open* in terms of the organization's relationships with its environment. Closed systems tend to minimize transactions with the environment and to take little account of external opinion in determining the purposes and activities of the organization. 'Closed systems are static or deterministic in their relations with their environment and in the interaction of their component parts. Their boundaries are set and tend to resist penetration' (Landers and Myers, 1977, p. 398). An example is the former primary school practice of exhorting parents to leave their children at the school gates but this is rare in the 1990s.

Open systems encourage interchanges with the environment, both responding to external influences and, in turn, seeking support for the objectives of the organization. In education, open systems theory shows the relationship between the institution and external groups such as parents, employers and the local education authority. Richman and Farmer (1974, p. 5) define open systems and point to their significance for the future of the institution: 'The organisation is viewed as transacting with external environmental elements with respect to the importing and exporting of money, people, energy, material, goods and services, information, and so on. . . . The exchange is an essential factor underlying the system's viability, its reproductive ability or continuity, and its ability to change.'

Educational institutions vary considerably in the extent to which they may be regarded as closed or open systems. Further education colleges have extensive and vital links with employers, who sponsor students on many part-time and some full-time courses, and with the FEFC and Training and Enterprise Councils which largely determine their levels of funding. Most schools may also be regarded as open systems because of the constant interaction with various groups and individuals in the neighbourhood. Selective schools and certain universities, which enjoy high reputations and which do not have to compete vigorously for students, may be sufficiently impervious to external influences to be categorized as closed systems.

The distinction between open and closed systems is more blurred in practice than it is in theory. It may be more useful to think of a continuum rather than a sharp distinction between polar opposites. All schools and colleges have a measure of interaction with their environments but the greater the dependence of the institution on external groups the more 'open' it is likely to be.

The educational reforms of the 1980s and 1990s, in Britain and elsewhere, have increased the salience of the open systems model. Schools have to compete for pupils and their income is tied closely to their levels of recruitment. To be attractive to potential parents, it is important to be responsive to their requirements. This can lead to permeable boundaries with parents and others influencing school policies and priorities. Hoy and Miskel (1987, p. 86) refer to the shift from closed to open systems:

> A closed systems model [is] not adequate for either illuminating or dealing with the pressing problems of educational administrators . . . organizations such as school systems are now viewed as open systems, which must adapt to changing external conditions to be effective and, in the long term, survive. The open system concept highlights the vulnerability and interdependence of organizations and their environments.

Systems theorists believe that organizations can be categorized as systems with their parts interacting to achieve systemic objectives. However, caution should be exercised in attributing these qualities to educational institutions. Schools and colleges are complex human organizations and systems models may be inadequate, as Hoyle (1981, p. 12) emphasizes: 'Schools are certainly not organisations consisting of carefully articulated parts functioning harmoniously in the pursuit of agreed objectives. They are characterised by conflict, malintegration and the pursuit of individual and group interests. Nevertheless a certain degree of systematic integration is necessary for their effective function.'

## Bureaucratic models

The bureaucratic model is probably the most important of the formal models. There is a substantial literature about its applicability to schools and colleges. It is often used broadly to refer to characteristics which are generic to formal organizations. Some writers suggest that bureaucracy is an almost inevitable consequence of increasing size and complexity. Livingstone (1974, p. 9), for example, argues that 'bureaucracy describes only the simple truth that as organisations grow and become more complex, more formal systems of regulation replace the informal understanding that is often sufficient for effective co-ordination in the smaller, simpler units'. The 'pure' version of the bureaucratic model is associated strongly with the work of Weber who argued that, in formal organizations, bureaucracy is the most efficient form of management:

> The purely bureaucratic type of administrative organization . . . is, from a technical point of view, capable of attaining the highest degree of efficiency and is in this sense formally the most rational means of carrying out imperative control over human beings. It is superior to any other form in precision, in stability, in the stringency of its discipline, and in its reliability.
> (Weber, 1989, p. 16)

Bureaucracy, then, describes a formal organization which seeks maximum efficiency through rational approaches to management. Its main features are as follows:

1. It stresses the importance of the *hierarchical authority structure* with formal chains of command between the different positions in the hierarchy. This pyramidal structure is based on the legal authority vested in the officers

who hold places in the chain of command. Office holders are responsible to superordinates for the satisfactory conduct of their duties. In educational institutions teachers are accountable to the head or principal.

2. In common with other formal models, the bureaucratic approach emphasizes the *goal orientation* of the organization. Institutions are dedicated to goals which are clearly delineated by the officers at the apex of the pyramid. In colleges or schools goals are determined largely by the principal or head and endorsed without question by other staff. 'Bureaucracy . . . has a common goal towards which members work under accepted leaders exercising legitimate authority . . . by virtue of office held at a particular time' (Ferguson 1980, p. 535).

3. The bureaucratic model suggests a *division of labour* with staff specializing in particular tasks on the basis of expertise. The departmental structure in secondary schools and colleges is an obvious manifestation of division of labour with subject specialists teaching a defined area of the curriculum. In this respect primary schools do not resemble bureaucracies because staff are typically class teachers who work with one group of children for much of their time.

4. In bureaucracies decisions and behaviour are governed by *rules and regulations* rather than personal initiative. Harling (1984, p. 8) points to the advantages of a formal and impersonal set of rules: 'The regulations ensure a degree of uniformity of operation and together with the authority structure make possible the coordination of the various activities. Such regulations provide a degree of continuity regardless of changes in personnel, thus promoting stability.' Schools typically have rules to regulate the behaviour of pupils and often guide the behaviour of teachers through bureaucratic devices such as the staff handbook.

5. Bureaucratic models emphasize *impersonal* relationships between staff and clients. This neutrality is designed to minimize the impact of individuality on decision-making. Good schools depend in part on the quality of personal relationships between teachers and pupils and this aspect of bureaucracy has little influence in many schools. Yet where schools require pupils to address staff as 'miss' or 'sir' they are promoting impersonal relationships and encouraging teachers to distance themselves from their students.

6. In bureaucracies the recruitment and career progress of staff are determined on *merit*. Appointments are made on the basis of qualifications and experience, and promotion depends on expertise demonstrated in present and previous positions. Schools and colleges fulfil this criterion in that formal competitive procedures are laid down for the appointment of new staff and for some promoted posts. Internal promotions, however, depend on the recommendation of the head or principal and there may be no formal process.

## Applying the bureaucratic model to education

All large organizations contain some bureaucratic elements and this is true of educational institutions:

Schools and colleges have many bureaucratic features, including a hierarchical structure with the headteacher or principal at the apex. Teachers specialise on the basis of expertise in secondary schools and colleges and, increasingly, in primary schools also. There are many rules for pupils and staff, whose working lives are largely dictated by 'the tyranny of the timetable'. Heads and senior staff are accountable to the governing body and external stakeholders for the activities of the school or college. Partly for these reasons, bureaucratic theories pervade much of the literature on educational management.

> (Bush, 1994, p. 36)

Hughes (1985, p. 8) concludes that the bureaucratic model applies to education: 'Schools and colleges, particularly if they are large, conform to a considerable degree to Weber's specification of bureaucracy, as judged by their division of work, their hierarchical structures, their rules and regulations, their impersonal procedures and their employment practices based on technical criteria.' The recognition that bureaucracy applies to many aspects of education is tempered by concern about its procedures becoming too dominant an influence on the operation of schools and colleges. There is a fear that the bureaucracy itself may become the *raison-d'être* of the organization rather than being firmly subordinated to educational aims:

> All schools are bureaucracies. There are rules governing the behaviour of the members. There is a hierarchy and there are formal and informal norms of behaviour associated with the various roles . . . One difficulty with a bureaucratic school system is that the bureaucracy and its survival become ends in themselves, and the goals of schooling become subsidiary.
>
> (Holmes and Wynne, 1989, pp. 63–4)

While not applicable in a pure form, the notion of bureaucracy provides powerful insights into the managerial processes and ideology of large parts of the education service. The management of our schools has been conditioned by both the ideology and practice of hierarchy and control to a point at which, in some cases, it must attract the pejorative term of *managerialism*, a condition under which the artificial needs of managers, organisations, systems, bureaucracies or routines assume dominance over the real needs of children.

> (Osborne, 1990, pp. 9–10)

Lunga (1985, p. 173) acknowledges these sceptical views but concludes that the bureaucratic model remains valid and appropriate for education: 'There is . . a formidable tradition that views bureaucracy in pejorative terms . . . bureaucracy as described by Weber is still the most appropriate form of organisation to facilitate the attainment of educational goals.'

The bureaucratic model has certain advantages for education but there are difficulties in applying it too enthusiastically to schools and colleges because of the centrality of their professional staff. 'If professional expertise is concentrated near the base of the bureaucratic pyramid the rules themselves must be largely a product of the consent of those to whom they apply. If this consent is not forthcoming the organisation risks fragmenting into competitive interest groups' (Williams and Blackstone, 1983, p. 94). We shall return to this issue in Chapter 4.

# Rational models

Rational approaches differ from other formal models in that they emphasize managerial *processes* rather than organizational structure or goals. The focus is on the process of decision-making instead of the structural framework which constrains but does not determine managerial decisions. This stress on process is the central element in Cuthbert's (1984, p. 39) definition of 'analytical-rational' models:

> Analytical-rational models are taken here to include all ideas of management as a process involving the rational and systematic analysis of situations, leading to identification and evaluation of possible courses of action, choice of a preferred alternative, implementation, and monitoring and review, in a cyclical repetitive process . . . The management process is depicted as a matter of systematic, informed, and rational decision-making.

Although the distinctive quality of rational models is their emphasis on process, they share several characteristics with the other formal theories. These include agreed organizational objectives and a bureaucratic organizational structure. The decision-making process thus takes place within a recognized structure and in pursuit of accepted goals.

The process of rational decision-making is thought to have the following sequence:

1. Perception of a problem or a choice opportunity.
2. Analysis of the problem, including data collection.
3. Formulation of alternative solutions or choices.
4. Choice of the most appropriate solution to the problem to meet the objectives of the organization.
5. Implementation of the chosen alternative.
6. Monitoring and evaluation of the effectiveness of the chosen strategy.

The process is essentially iterative in that the evaluation may lead to a redefinition of the problem or a search for an alternative solution (see Figure 3.2).

In Chapter 2 we noted that theories tend to be *normative* in that they reflect views about how organizations and individuals ought to behave. The rational model is certainly normative in that it presents an idealized view of the decision-making process. It has serious limitations as a portrayal of the decision-making process in education:

- There may be dispute over objectives and the definition of the 'problem' is likely to be dependent on the particular standpoint of the individuals involved.
- Some of the data needed to make a decision may not be available.
- Most problematic of all is the assumption that the choice of solution can be detached and impartial. In practice, individuals and groups are likely to promote their own favoured solutions which in turn may reflect individual rather than organizational objectives.
- The perceived effectiveness of the chosen solution may also vary according to the preferences of the people concerned.

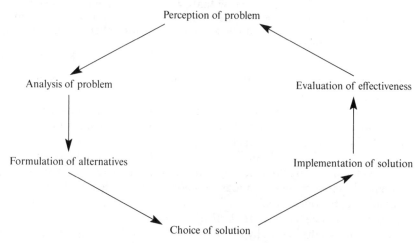

**Figure 3.2** The rational process

Despite these practical limitations, the rational model remains the basis for much of the analysis of decision-making in education, notably in respect of strategic planning (West-Burnham, 1994) and financial resource allocation (Coleman, Bush and Glover, 1994; Davies, 1994). Ellstrom (1983, p. 233) is right to claim that 'in spite of the severe criticism that has been levelled against the rational model and its derivatives, its fundamental elements have, to a large extent, been retained as the predominant mode of organisational analysis'.

## Hierarchical models

Hierarchical approaches stress vertical relationships within organizations and the accountability of leaders to external sponsors. The organizational structure is emphasized with particular reference to the authority and responsibility of the managers at the apex of the structure. Packwood (1977, p. 1) refers to the prevalence of the hierarchy in formal organizations and explains its significance:

> the hierarchy is the general structure in all developed cultures for achieving work objectives that are beyond the control of the single individual. Through a series of manager-subordinate relationships it explicitly locates accountability for work. The manager in the hierarchy is accountable not only for his, or her, performance, but also for the work of subordinates.

Packwood returned to his support for hierarchy twelve years after his previous article. He provides a precise definition of the hierarchical model and locates it firmly within the bureaucratic framework:

> One of the basic properties of bureaucratic organisation is the way in which occupational roles are graded in a vertical hierarchy. Authority to prescribe work passes from senior to junior roles, while accountability for the performance of work passes in the reverse direction from junior to senior. Authority and accountability are impersonal in that they are attached to roles,

not to the personalities of the individuals who occupy the roles. The head-teacher has authority to define the work of the deputy headteacher in a school because he or she occupies the role of headteacher not because of who he or she is as an individual.

(Packwood, 1989, pp. 9–10)

This view subordinates individuals to the organizational hierarchy. Subjective theorists are very critical of this stance as we shall see in Chapter 6.

In hierarchical models the organization structure is depicted as *pyramidal* with authority located at the top of the structure. Educational institutions are often typified in this way, as Lortie (1969, p. 4) suggests: 'The formal and legal allocation of authority in school systems is monolithic, hierarchical and concentrated; official powers are focused at the apex of the structure. A system of this kind implies that those in command set goals, oversee their realisation, and are accountable for outcomes.'

Hierarchical models emphasize *vertical communication* patterns. Information is passed down the hierarchy to all appropriate levels and subordinates are expected to implement the decisions made by the senior managers. Difficult issues may be referred upwards until they reach a level where they can be resolved. In schools and colleges the head or principal is thought to inform heads of department or other staff about policies and is the final arbiter of problems incapable of resolution at lower levels in the hierarchy.

Horizontal communication also plays a part in the hierarchy but Packwood (1989) argues that such contacts are for co-ordination rather than management. The curriculum co-ordinator role in primary schools is an example of a lateral relationship. Co-ordinators communicate with class teachers about aspects of their subject but they do not have managerial authority over them.

Central to hierarchical models is the concept of *accountability*. Leaders are responsible to external agencies for the performance of subordinates and the activities of the organization. In schools, the accountability of heads to the governing body, and to the LEA or FAS, is a major bulwark of their authority. Marriott (1981) claims that the junior school head has 'supreme legitimate authority' while Taylor (1983) asserts that 'ultimate responsibility for a school's performance resides with the head'.

Harling (1980) points to five areas where the primary head tends to have the decisive role:

1. determination of the overall aims of the school;
2. allocation of human and material resources;
3. control of internal and external communications;
4. formulation of school rules and regulations;
5. evaluation of staff and pupil progress.

The overarching role of primary school heads is modified in secondary schools and colleges where their sheer size limits the personal involvement of heads and principals. Mortimore and Mortimore's (1991, p. 168) research on secondary heads shows the extent to which they have used the hierarchy to delegate tasks and the substantial degree of discretion they have in determining the management structure of the school:

We have been struck by the amount of thought and effort the headteachers put into the organization and management of schools. The size and complexity of the schools and the wide-ranging responsibilities carried out by today's headteachers necessitates a considerable degree of delegation. Different management structures have been devised, according to the priorities and preferred management styles of the heads.

Hierarchical models have certain limitations when applied to educational institutions. Teachers as professionals claim discretion in their classroom work and there is increasing participation in decision-making on wider school issues. As a result 'the several strands of hierarchical control, collegial control, and autonomy become tangled and complex' (Lortie, 1969, p. 1).

Some further education colleges have acknowledged the weaknesses of the hierarchy by introducing matrix structures (FESC, 1989). These generally emphasize lateral relationships and the primacy of course teams but the structure often lacks the clarity associated with hierarchy. For this reason, and because of the clear legal authority of the principal, hierarchical models cannot be dismissed as irrelevant for self-managing schools and colleges.

## Formal models: goals, structure, environment and leadership

### Goals

Formal models characterize schools and colleges as *goal oriented*. There is an assumption that institutions pursue specific objectives. These goals are invariably determined by heads and senior staff and formal theories do not regard the support of other teachers as problematic. All members of the organization are thought to be working towards the achievement of these official aims. Everard and Morris (1990, pp. 149 and 151) stress the significance of goals:

> We believe that all organizations, including educational ones, should be actively managed against goals; in other words, not only should there be a clear sense of direction in which the organization is being steered, but also markers whereby we can assess progress . . . Organizational aims . . . nurture and steer creative tension and release and harness human energy; they keep the organization on the move, heading in a certain direction.

The activities and procedures of institutions are evaluated in terms of their relevance to the approved objectives, as Harling (1984, p. 7) suggests: 'The distinctive characteristic of an organisation is . . . that it has been formally established for the explicit purpose of achieving certain goals. Every organisation has a formally instituted pattern of authority and an official body of rules and procedures which are intended to aid the achievement of those goals.' The problem is that official goals are often so nebulous that they offer little guidance to action. When Barry Bainbridge took up the headship of Pensnett School in 1986, he received a copy of the school's aims. 'There was nothing to take exception to. The aims were so vague and wordy, I couldn't disagree with them. It is the interpretation of the aims which is critical' (Bush, 1988, p. 23).

The portrayal of schools and colleges as organizations actively pursuing official goals set out in formal statements is modified by certain writers who acknowledge the existence of multiple objectives in institutions: 'Organizations usually have more than one objective . . . schools that make their aims explicit usually find that they are having to harmonize different though compatible aims' (Everard and Morris, 1990, p. 152). The diverse goals of schools and colleges often emanate from different parts of the organization. Beck and Cox (1984), for example, distinguish between personal goals, team goals and organizational goals. Similarly Livingstone (1974) differentiates between individual, departmental and formal goals. In a secondary school an official goal may refer to the fulfilment of the potential of all pupils. A departmental goal might relate to the attainment of particular standards of competence in certain subjects. Individual goals may well reflect personal career ambitions.

Despite the recognition that goals may exist at different levels, there remains the clear implication that personal and subunit goals should be subordinated to the official aims. Everard and Morris (1990, p. 152), for example, argue that the aims of constituent parts of the school; departments, teams and committees, 'should be kept aligned with those of the school'. This assumption underpins the notion of development planning in schools and colleges where subunit plans are expected to be consistent with those of the institutional level.

The belief that it is the organization's official goals that guide the behaviour and decisions of staff may be unrealistic or naive. As we shall see in subsequent chapters, formal goals may be contested or provide only a limited guide to action.

## Organizational structure

Formal models present organizational *structure* as an objective fact. Schools and colleges are 'real' institutions which imbue teachers and pupils with a sense of belonging. Staff are thought to define their professional lives in terms of their position within the school or college. Structures may be typified in physical terms that imply permanence (see Figure 3.1). Individuals are accorded a place in the structure such as teacher of class 2 or head of the physics department. The work of teachers and other staff is defined in terms of their roles within the formal structure. The structure is assumed to influence the behaviour of the individuals holding particular roles in the organization. Structure dominates and individuality is de-emphasized: 'The role structure remains relatively stable whilst different incumbents of the roles come and go' (Hoyle, 1986, p. 5).

## The external environment

Formal approaches differ in the way they typify relationships between the organization and its environment. The more rigid models, such as 'closed systems' or structural theories, tend to limit environmental links to the minimum required to sustain accountability. These perspectives characterize relationships in terms of the official links between the head or principal and such formal groups as the LEA and the governing body. Interaction with other groups, such as parents, employers and other educational institutions, is de-emphasized. 'Closed systems' models assume that schools or colleges are impervious to such influences.

Other formal models, such as 'open systems', postulate wide-ranging links with the environment. Educational institutions are portrayed as interactive organizations, responding to a changing environment and displaying their achievements to the local community. Everard and Morris (1990, pp. 155–6) stress the need for schools and colleges to be responsive to the wider system:

> Those who manage organizations should remember that they are part of a bigger system; they are interdependent with the rest of society, which they serve as society serves them . . . Many long-serving heads . . . have remarked how much . . . the nature of their jobs has changed to one of boundary management: that is they spend much more of their time managing transactions between the school and its environment.

Two schools studied by the author in the late 1980s both provide good examples of 'open systems'. Wroxham primary school has extensive links with external groups and individuals, particularly parents, as Frances Smith, the headteacher, explains: 'You can't really work with children successfully in a school unless you have parents' co-operation and understanding . . . it's very important that parents are very much involved in school life' (Bush, 1988, p. 30).

The Pensnett comprehensive school was designated a community school in 1986 when a purpose-built neighbourhood centre was opened on the school site. 'The school's extensive links with the community suggest an "open system". There is a community element in the upper-school core curriculum, with pupils spending part of their time working with local groups' (Bush, 1988, p. 31).

In the competitive climate engendered by the Education Reform Act and subsequent legislation, schools and colleges are increasingly adopting a more 'open' stance, conscious of the need for a good reputation with present and prospective parents, employers and the local community. Few educational institutions justify the label 'closed' in the 1990s.

## Leadership

Within formal models *leadership* is ascribed to the person at the apex of the hierarchy. It is assumed that this individual sets the tone of the organization and establishes the major official objectives. Baldridge *et al.* (1978, p. 44) discuss the nature of formal leadership:

> Under the bureaucratic model the leader is seen as the hero who stands at the top of a complex pyramid of power. The hero's job is to assess the problems, consider alternatives, and make rational choices. Much of the organisation's power is held by the hero, and great expectations are raised because people trust him [*sic*] to solve problems and fend off threats from the environment.

The leader is expected to play a key part in policy-making, and adoption of innovations is assumed to follow. The possibility of opposition, or indifference, to change is not acknowledged. It is believed that implementation is unproblematic: 'This is not to say that others, further down the hierarchy, will not require information and explanation, nor that there will not be problems, but that the flow of information is down the hierarchy and is dependent upon acceptance of a policy, plan or decision at the top' (Hewton, 1982, p. 35). In education there are several features that support this characteristic of unidimensional leadership. Official bodies and individuals behave as if the head or principal is the fount of all knowledge and authority. The head is the focal point for most external communications, and parents and community leaders generally expect to contact the school via the head. Many other groups tend to regard the head or principal as the public face of the institution and behave accordingly.

In primary schools, in particular, there is a perceived identity between the head and the school which reinforces the 'top down' perspective on leadership. 'Because of his [*sic*] formal authority the head represents and symbolises the school both to people inside it and to members of the community' (Coulson, 1985, p. 9). The staff of Wroxham primary school tend to reinforce this 'top-down' perspective on leadership, as the following comments illustrate:

'The head has overall responsibility for the school and everything in it'.

'The headteacher is the main establisher of policy – that's right because she is accountable'.

'The head has to carry the can'.

(Bush, 1988, p. 32)

These views are echoed by a teacher at St Meryl Primary School in Oxhey, near Watford, who uses a naval analogy to illustrate the head's role:

[The head] is the leader, almost the captain of a ship and we are the crew. She can tap into knowledge from the governors, from the teaching staff, from Herts. county council. She has knowledge of all these things which I don't have so I trust her decisions in the end.

(Bush, 1993, p. 28)

The head of Churchfields comprehensive school in the West Midlands aspires to a collegial approach, as we shall see in Chapter 4, but the need for accountability to external groups means that the head may operate as a 'top-down' leader in certain circumstances:

'He is probably the one person who is in the best position to be able to oversee the school as a whole. I think it is right and proper that most decisions should come from the top otherwise you get nothing done. Somebody has to carry the can at the end of the day. I think if he is being paid the money he should be doing it'.

(Head of Department, quoted by Bush, 1993, p. 39)

The assumption of an all-powerful leader at the apex of schools and colleges has several limitations. While formal authority resides with heads, they require the consent of colleagues if policy initiatives are to be carried through into departmental and classroom practice. It is now a truism that staff must 'own' decisions if they are to be implemented successfully.

Heads of self-managing schools and colleges have to share power with other staff in order to cope with the sheer volume of work arising from their enhanced responsibility for managing finance, staff and external relations. This pragmatic response to change serves to modify the notion of all-powerful heads but in many cases the effect has been to increase the role of the senior management team and not to empower more junior staff. The hierarchy remains intact but the apex comprises a team rather than a single individual (Wallace and Hall, 1994).

## The limitations of formal models

The various formal models pervade much of the literature on educational management. They are normative approaches in that they present ideas about how people in organizations *ought* to behave. So schools and colleges are typified as goal-seeking organizations employing rational means to achieve the objectives established by official leaders. Packwood (1989, p. 9) argues that the dramatic changes of recent years serve to increase the significance of formal models:

> The last decade has also seen fundamental changes in the way in which education is provided . . . many of these changes can only be understood and accommodated in the context of a bureaucratic theory of educational organisation . . . If schools are to make the best of the new demands that have, to a great extent, been imposed upon them, they have no choice but to make the best of bureaucracy.

Packwood seems to be arguing that because a top-down model is operating in imposing change on schools and colleges, their leaders should respond by managing their establishments in the same way. Yet for staff of educational institutions this framework seems inadequate. As one experienced secondary head suggests, 'there is the greatest discrepancy between the declared rational process and the undeclared, often unperceived, reality' (Marland, 1982).

Formal models are selective as well as normative. In focusing on the bureaucratic and structural aspects of organizations they necessarily ignore or underestimate other salient features. Several writers refer to the weaknesses of formal models:

> [Formal approaches] have limited our view of what an organisation is and how it operates.
>
> (Griffiths, 1978, p. 80)

> Models of classical management theory provide only a first approximation to an understanding of school organisation.
>
> (Hughes, 1978, p. 239)

> Rationalistic-bureaucratic notions . . . have largely proven to be sterile and to have little application to administrative practice in the 'real world'.
>
> (Owens and Shakeshaft, 1992, p. 4)

There are five specific weaknesses associated with formal models:

1. It may be unrealistic to characterize schools and colleges as *goal-oriented* organizations. It is often difficult to ascertain the goals of educational institutions. Formal objectives may have little operational relevance, as Perrow (1961, p. 855) suggests:

   > Official goals are purposely vague and general and do not indicate two major factors which influence organisational behaviour: the host of decisions that must be made among alternative ways of achieving official goals and the priority of multiple goals, and the many unofficial goals pursued by groups within the organisation. . . . [These] operative goals designate the ends sought through the actual operating policies of the organisation; they tell us what the organisation actually is trying to do, regardless of what the official goals say are the aims.

The introduction of development planning in the 1990s has led to the identification of specific aims in many schools. This, generally short-term, planning is consistent with the formal model and lends support to the notion of 'goal-seeking' organizations. However, development planning does not usually deal with all aspects of school life but only those priorities identified at a particular time.

Even where the purposes of schools and colleges have been clarified, there are further problems in judging whether objectives have been achieved. Many of the goals associated with education are very difficult to measure. The hostility to the British government's league tables relates in part to their limitations as measures of school effectiveness while the search for 'value-added' criteria has yet to produce widely accepted outcomes.

2. The portrayal of decision-making as a *rational* process is fraught with difficulties. The belief that managerial action is preceded by a process of evaluation of alternatives and a considered choice of the most appropriate option is rarely substantiated. Decisions in schools and colleges are made by teachers, who draw on a whole range of experience as they respond to events. Much human behaviour is irrational and this inevitably influences the nature of decision-making in education. Weick (1976, p. 1) asserts that rational practice is the exception rather than the norm:

> People in organisations, including educational organisations, find themselves hard pressed either to find actual instances of those rational practices or to find rationalised practices whose outcomes have been as beneficent as predicted, or to feel that those rational occasions explain much of what goes on within the organisation. Parts of some organisations are heavily rationalised but many parts also prove intractable to analysis through rational assumptions.

Educational institutions, in common with other organizations staffed by professionals, depend on decisions made by individuals and subunits. Professional judgement is based as much on the expertise of the individual as on rational processes conditioned by the rule book.

3. Formal models focus on the organization as an entity and ignore or underestimate the contribution of *individuals*. They assume that people occupy preordained positions in the structure and that their behaviour reflects their organizational positions rather than their individual qualities and experience. Critics argue that formal perspectives treat organizations as if they are independent of the people within them. Greenfield (1973, p. 571) has been particularly critical of this view:

> Most theories of organisation grossly simplify the nature of the reality with which they deal. The drive to see the organisation as a single kind of entity with a life of its own apart from the perceptions and beliefs of those involved in it blinds us to its complexity and the variety of organisations people create around themselves.

Greenfield's alternative approach to organizations is discussed in Chapter 6 but the essence of his argument is that organizations are the creation of the people within them. He claims that formal models greatly underestimate individual variables and thus produce an inaccurate portrayal of schools and colleges.

4. A central assumption of formal models is that power resides at the apex of the pyramid. Heads and principals possess authority by virtue of their positions as the appointed leaders of their institutions. This focus on official authority leads to a view of institutional management which is essentially *top down*. Policy is laid down by senior managers and implemented by staff lower down the hierarchy. Their acceptance of managerial decisions is regarded as unproblematic.

The hierarchical aspect of the formal model is most relevant to organizations which depend on tight discipline for their effectiveness. The armed forces, for example, are expected to carry out their orders without any questioning or elaboration. The situation is assumed to require compliance with instructions from superordinates.

Organizations with large numbers of professional staff tend to exhibit signs of tension between the conflicting demands of professionalism and the hierarchy. Formal models assume that leaders, because they are appointed on merit, have the competence to issue appropriate instructions to subordinates. This is supported by the authority vested in them by virtue of their official position. Professional organizations have a rather different ethos with expertise distributed widely within the institution. Osborne (1990, p. 10) refers to the conflict between professionalism and bureaucracy: 'The great weight of evidence is that the employment of large numbers of professionals in an organisation poses "problems" for the application of the bureaucratic or hierarchical model.'

Where professionals specialize, as in secondary schools and colleges, the ability of leaders to direct the actions of subordinates may be questionable. A head who is a humanities graduate lacks the specific competence to supervise teaching in the faculty of technology. In professional organizations there is an authority of expertise which may come into conflict with positional authority. Hughes (1978, p. 240) discusses this paradox:

It is through the independent exercise of his trained judgement, irrespective of his formal position, that the expert makes his contribution to an organisation. It is through precisely the same activity that the expert comes into conflict with the administrative hierarchy. Furthermore, it is unsafe to assume under all circumstances that technical expertise necessarily, or even generally, increases with position in the formal hierarchy.

Heads are responsible for the quality of the teaching process in their school, particularly in the light of the National Curriculum and the OFSTED inspection regime introduced in the 1990s. However, their authority over teachers may be ambiguous. Professional staff claim zones of autonomy based on their specialist expertise. The classroom is still largely the domain of the teacher and pedagogic matters are primarily the responsibility of the practitioner as a qualified professional. These areas of discretion may lead to conflict between heads and other staff. Such difficulties can be avoided only if there is at least tacit acceptance of the head's overall responsibility for the activities of the school. This involves the recognition by teachers of the head's right to take the initiative in many areas of school policy. Teachers do generally concede authority to the head as we noted earlier (page 44).

5. *Formal approaches are based on the implicit assumption that organizations are relatively* stable. Individuals may come and go but they slot into pre-determined positions in a static structure. Bureaucratic and structural theories are most appropriate in stable conditions as Bolman and Deal (1984, p. 57) suggest: 'The structural frame helps to capture the more stable and formal aspects of human behaviour in organisations.' It can be argued that assumptions of stability are unrealistic in many organizations and invalid in most schools and colleges. March and Olsen (1976, p. 21) are right to claim that 'Individuals find themselves in a more complex, less stable and less understood world than that described by standard theories of organisational choice'. Rational perspectives require a measure of predictability to be useful as portrayals of organizational behaviour. The validity of formal models may be limited during phases of rapid and multiple change, such as the post Education Reform Act period in England and Wales. The notion of a thorough analysis of a problem followed by identification of alternatives, choice of the preferred option and a process of implementation and evaluation may be unrealistic during periods of turbulence.

## Conclusion: are formal models still valid?

These criticisms of formal models suggest that they have serious limitations in respect of schools and colleges. The dominance of the hierarchy is compromised by the expertise possessed by professional staff. The supposed rationality of the decision-making process requires modification to allow for the pace and complexity of change. The concept of organizational goals is challenged by those who point to the existence of multiple objectives in education and the possible conflict between goals held at individual, departmental and institutional levels.

Despite these limitations, it would be inappropriate to dismiss formal approaches as irrelevant to schools and colleges. The other models discussed in this book were all developed as a reaction to the perceived weaknesses of formal theories. However, these alternative perspectives have not succeeded in dislodging the formal models which remain valid as *partial* descriptions of organization and management in education. As Harling (1984) suggests: 'the purely formal models are inadequate but certainly not defunct'. Owens and Shakeshaft (1992) refer to a reduction of confidence in bureaucratic models and a 'paradigm shift' to a more sophisticated analysis. In subsequent chapters we examine several alternative perspectives and assess the extent to which they have supplanted formal models as the principal means of understanding and managing schools and colleges.

## References

Baldridge, J. V., Curtis, D. V., Ecker, G. and Riley, G. L. (1978) *Policy-Making and Effective Leadership*, Jossey Bass, San Francisco.

Becher, T. and Kogan, M. (1992) *Process and Structure in Higher Education*, Routledge, London.

Beck, J. and Cox, C. (1984) Developing organisational skills, in C. Cox and J. Beck (eds.) *Management Development: Advances in Practice and Theory*, John Wiley, New York.

Bolman, L. G. and Deal, T. E. (1984) *Modern Approaches to Understanding and Managing Organisations*, Jossey Bass, San Francisco.

Brannen, R., Holloway, D and Peeke, G. (1981) Departmental organisational structures in further education, *Journal of Further and Higher Education*, Vol. 5, no. 3, pp. 22–32.

Bush, T. (1988) *Action and Theory in School Management*, E325 Managing Schools, The Open University, Milton Keynes.

Bush, T. (1989) School management structures – theory and practice, *Educational Management and Administration*, Vol. 17, no. 1, pp. 3–8, Winter.

Bush, T. (1993) *Exploring Collegiality: Theory, Process and Structure*, E326 Managing Schools: Challenge and Response, The Open University, Milton Keynes.

Bush, T. (1994) Theory and practice in educational management, in T. Bush and J. West-Burnham (eds.) *The Principles of Educational Management*, Longman, Harlow.

Clark, B. R. (1983) The contradictions of change in academic systems, *Higher Education*, Vol. 12, pp. 101–16.

Coleman, M., Bush, T. and Glover, D. (1994) *Managing Finance and External Relations*, Longman, Harlow.

Coulson, A. (1985) *The Managerial Behaviour of Primary School Heads*, Collected Original Resources in Education, Carfax Publishing Company, Abingdon.

Cuthbert, R. (1984) *The Management Process*, E324 Management in Post Compulsory Education, Block 3, Part 2, The Open University Press, Milton Keynes.

Davies, B. (1994) Models of decision-making in resource allocation, in T. Bush and J. West-Burnham (eds.) *The Principles of Educational Management*, Longman, Harlow.

Ellstrom, P. E. (1983) Four faces of educational organisations, *Higher Education*, Vol. 12, pp. 231–41.

Everard, B. and Morris, G. (1990) *Effective School Management*, Paul Chapman Publishing, London.

Ferguson, C. (1980) Alternative organisational structures in higher and further education, *Coombe Lodge Report*, Vol. 12, no. 12, pp. 535–72.

Further Education Staff College (1989), FESC 1987 survey result published, *Coombe Lodge Report*, Vol. 21, no. 2, pp. 535–72.

Greenfield, T. B. (1973) Organisations as social inventions: rethinking assumptions about change, *Journal of Applied Behavioural Science*, Vol. 9, no. 5, pp. 551–74.

Greenfield T. B. (1975) Theory about organisation: a new perspective and its implications for schools, in M. Hughes (ed.) *Administering Education: International Challenge*, Athlone Press, London.

Griffiths, D. E. (1978) Contemporary theory development and educational administration, *Educational Administration*, Vol. 6, no. 2, pp. 80–93.

Harling, P. (1980) School decision-making and the primary headteacher, *Education, 3–13*, Vol. 8, no. 2, pp. 44–8.

Harling, P. (1984) The organisational framework for educational leadership, in P. Harling (ed.) *New Directions in Educational Leadership*, Falmer Press, Lewes.

Newton, E. (1982) *Rethinking Educational Change*, Society for Research into Higher Education, Guildford.

Holmes, M. and Wynne, E. (1989) *Making the School an Effective Community: Belief, Practice and Theory in School Administration*, The Falmer Press, Lewes.

Hoy, W. and Miskel, C. (1987) *Educational Administration: Theory, Research and Practice*, McGraw-Hill, New York.

Hoyle, E. (1981) *The Process of Management*, E323 Management and the School, Block 3, Part 1, Open University Press, Milton Keynes.

Hoyle, E. (1986) *The Politics of School Management*, Hodder and Stoughton, Sevenoaks.

Hughes, M. G. (1978) Reconciling professional and administrative concerns, Commonwealth Council For Educational Administration, *Studies in Educational Administration*, 13

Hughes, M. (1985) Theory and practice in educational management, in M. Hughes, P. Ribbins and H. Thomas (eds.) *Managing Education: The System and the Institution*, Holt, Rinehart and Winston, London.

Landers, T. J. and Myers, J. G. (1977) *Essentials of Schools Management*, W. B. Saunders, Philadelphia.

Latcham, J. and Cuthbert, R. (1983) A systems approach to college management, in O. Boyd-Barrett, T. Bush, J. Goodey, I McNay and M. Preedy (eds.) *Approaches to Post-School Management*, Harper and Row, London.

Livingstone, H. (1974) *The University: An Organisational Analysis*, Blackie, Glasgow.

Lortie, D. C. (1969) The balance of control and autonomy in elementary school teaching, in A. Etzioni (ed.) *The Semi-Professions and Their Organisation*, Free Press, a division of Macmillan, Inc., New York.

Lungu, G. (1985) In defence of bureaucratic organisation in education, *Educational Management and Administration*, Vol. 13, pp. 172–8.

March, J. G. and Olsen, J. P. (1976) Organisational choice under ambiguity, in J. G. March and J. P. Olsen, *Ambiguity and Choice in Organisations*, Universitetsforlaget, Bergen.

Marland, M. (1982) The politics of improvement in schools, *Educational Management and Administration*, Vol. 10, no. 2, pp. 119–34.

Marriott, S. (1981) Patterns of authority and autonomy in three junior schools, *Durham and Newcastle Research Review*, Vol. 9, no. 47, pp. 269–78.

Moran, W. E. (1972) A systems view of university organisation, in P. W. Hamelman (ed.) *Managing the University: A Systems Approach*, Praeger, New York.

Mortimore, P. and Mortimore, J. (1991) *The Secondary Head: Roles, Responsibilities and Reflections*, Paul Chapman Publishing, London.

Osborne, A. (1990) The nature of educational management, in B. Davies, L. Ellison, A. Osborne and J. West-Burnham (eds.) *Education Management for the 1990s*, Longman, Harlow.

Owens, R. and Shakeshaft, C. (1992) The new 'revolution' in administrative theory, *Journal of Educational Management*, Vol. 30, no. 9, pp. 4–17.

Packwood, T. (1977) The school as a hierarchy, *Educational Administration*, Vol. 5, no. 2, pp. 1–6.

Packwood, T. (1989) Return to the hierarchy, *Educational Management and Administration*, Vol. 17, no. 1, pp. 9–15, Winter.

Perrow, C. (1961) The analysis of goals in complex organisations, *American Sociological Review*, Vol. 26, pp. 854–6.

Renshaw, P. (1974) Education and the primary school – a contradiction? *Education for Teaching*, Vol. 93, pp. 8–16.

Richman, B. M. and Farmer, R. N. (1974) *Leadership, Goals and Power in Higher Education*, Jossey Bass, San Francisco.

Silverman, D. (1970) *The Theory of Organisations*, Gower, Aldershot.

Taylor, K. (1983) Heads and the freedom to manage, *School Organisation*, Vol. 3, no. 3, pp. 273–86.

Wallace, M. and Hall, V. (1994), *Inside the SMT: Teamwork in Secondary School Management*, Paul Chapman Publishing, London.

Weber, M. (1947) in T. Parsons (ed.) *The Theory of Social and Economic Organisation*, Free Press, Glencoe, Illinois and Collier-Macmillan, New York.

Weber, M. (1989) Legal authority in a bureaucracy, in T. Bush (ed.) *Managing Education: Theory and Practice*, Open University Press, Milton Keynes.

Weick, K. E. (1976) Educational organisations as loosely coupled systems, *Administrative Science Quarterly*, Vol. 21, no. 1, pp. 1–19.

West-Burnham, J. (1994) Strategy, policy and planning, in T. Bush and J. West-Burnham (eds.) *The Principles of Educational Management*, Longman, Harlow.

Williams, G. and Blackstone, T. (1983) *Response to Adversity*, Society for Research into Higher Education, Guildford.

# 4

# *Collegial Models*

## Central features of collegial models

Collegial models include all those theories which emphasize that power and decision-making should be shared among some or all members of the organization. These approaches range from a 'restricted' collegiality where the leader shares power with a limited number of senior colleagues to a 'pure' collegiality where all members have an equal voice in determining policy. The definition suggested below captures the main features of these perspectives:

> Collegial models assume that organizations determine policy and make decisions through a process of discussion leading to consensus. Power is shared among some or all members of the organization who are thought to have a mutual understanding about the objectives of the institution.

The notion of collegiality has become enshrined in the folklore of management as the most appropriate way to run schools and colleges in the 1990s. It has become closely associated with school effectiveness and school improvement (Campbell and Southworth, 1993) and is increasingly regarded as 'the official model of good practice' (Wallace, 1989, p. 182). Campbell (1985, pp. 152–3) refers to the trend towards collegiality in primary education:

> The contemporary image of good practice has been promoted by the Inspectorate since 1978 . . . It is of the 'collegial' primary school, predicated on the two values of teacher collaboration and subject expertise . . . It shows small working groups of teachers reporting back recommendations for school-wide change to the collectivity of the whole staff meeting for decision taking. These groups are led and organised by the curriculum postholders who draw upon expertise from outside school as well as upon their own professional knowledge, in order to enable the staff to develop the curriculum as authoritatively as possible . . . Supporting this collaborative effort is the headteacher who has committed himself or herself to devolving responsibility to the staff group.

Little (1990, p. 166) discusses the benefits of collegiality:

> The reason to pursue the study and practice of collegiality is that, presumably, something is gained when teachers work together and something is lost

when they do not; in effect, the perceived benefits must be great enough that the time teachers spend together can compete with time spent in other ways, on other priorities that are equally compelling or more immediate.

The time required to implement collegial approaches is a significant constraint as we shall see later in this chapter (pp. 67).

Collegial models have the following major features:

1. They are strongly *normative* in orientation. We noted in Chapter 2 that all theories tend to be normative but collegial approaches in particular reflect the prescriptive view that management ought to be based on agreement. Their advocates believe that decision-making should be based on demo-cratic principles but do not necessarily claim that these principles actually determine the nature of management in action. It is an idealistic model rather than one that is founded firmly in practice:

> Those who advocate collegiality do so on the basis of prescription rather than description [but] . . . it may not be simply an act of faith.
> (Campbell and Southworth, 1993, p. 62)

> [Collegiality] is a projection from empirical reality, not a description of it.
> (Campbell, 1985, p. 153)

2. Collegial models seem to be particularly appropriate for organizations such as schools and colleges that have significant numbers of professional staff. Teachers possess authority arising directly from their knowledge and skill. They have an *authority of expertise* that contrasts with the positional authority associated with formal models. Professional auth-ority occurs where decisions are made on an individual basis rather than being standardized. Education necessarily demands a professional ap-proach because pupils and students need personal attention. Teachers require a measure of autonomy in the classroom but also need to collabo-rate to ensure a coherent approach to teaching and learning. Collegial models assume that professionals also have a right to share in the wider decision-making process:

> The claim inherent in professionalism to self-determination in the ex-ercise of professional functions was extended beyond the areas of strictly professional competence into the sphere of general organisational plan-ning and its detailed execution. The extension of the dominant profes-sional ethic to the administration of a large organisation implied the right of status equals to be respected and consulted
> (Noble and Pym, 1970, p. 433)

. Collegial models assume a *common set of values* held by members of the organization. These may arise from the socialization which occurs during training and the early years of professional practice. These common values guide the managerial activities of the organization and in particular are thought to lead to shared educational objectives. Campbell and Southworth (1993, p. 66) refer to 'jointly held beliefs and values' in reporting their study of staff relationships in primary schools.

The common values of professionals form part of the justification for the optimistic assumption that it is always possible to reach agreement about goals and policies. According to Richman and Farmer (1974, p. 29), the collegial model

> has a very strong harmony bias that assumes away the possibility of conflict. It is only likely to work well . . . where virtually all of the participants – especially the more active ones – have a strong spirit of genuine co-operation, similar values and personal goals, and a deep commitment to the institution and its goals and priorities.

4. The *size* of decision-making groups is an important element in collegial management. They have to be sufficiently small to enable everyone to be heard. This may mean that collegiality works better in primary schools or in subunits than at the institutional level in secondary schools and colleges. Meetings of the whole staff may operate collegially in small schools but may be suitable only for information exchange in larger institutions.

The collegial model deals with this problem of scale by building-in the assumption that staff have *formal representation* within the various decision-making bodies. Significant areas of policy are determined within the official committee system rather than being a prerogative of individual leaders. The democratic element of formal representation rests on the allegiance owed by participants to their constituencies. A teacher representing the English department on a committee is accountable to colleagues who may have the right to nominate or elect another person if they are not happy about the way they are being represented.

Informal consultations with staff do not constitute collegiality. Where heads seek the advice of colleagues before making a decision the process is one of consultation whereas the essence of collegiality is participation in decision-making. Power is shared with staff in a democracy rather than remaining the preserve of the leader. Formal representation confers the right to participate in defined areas of policy while informal consultation is at the sole discretion of the leader who is under no obligation to act on the advice received.

5. Collegial models assume that decisions are reached by *consensus* rather than division or conflict. The belief that there are common values and shared objectives leads to the view that it is both desirable and possible to resolve problems by agreement. There may be differences of opinion but they can be overcome by the force of argument. The decision-making process may be elongated by the search for compromise but this is regarded as an acceptable price to pay to maintain the aura of shared values and beliefs. This ethic of consensus is stressed by Moodie and Eustace (1974, p. 221):

> the ideal of rule by consensus underlines the important and widespread feeling that, at least with respect to major policy decisions, no simple majoritarian system can successfully be operated . . . Instead the stress is placed upon discussion and persuasion as the proper means to securing agreement upon the most important decisions.

The case for consensual decision-making rests in part on the ethical dimension of collegiality. It is regarded as wholly appropriate to involve people in the decisions which affect their professional lives. Imposing decisions on staff is considered morally repugnant and inconsistent with the notion of consent. Williams (1989, p. 80) outlines this moral argument:

> The moral character of an exercise of authority is based on the presence of consent on the part of those subject to its jurisdiction . . . the consent of the obligated is necessary for authority to assume moral status . . . Where consent is not made a condition of authority, then we are not speaking of moral authority, but of the exercise of power, or of purely formal or legal authority.

These five central features of collegiality appear to a greater or lesser extent in each of the main sectors of education. We turn now to consider its application in higher education.

## Collegial models in higher education

Collegial approaches in British education originated within the colleges of Oxford and Cambridge universities (Becher and Kogan, 1992, p. 72): 'Collegium designates a structure or structures in which members have equal authority to participate in decisions which are binding on each of them. It usually implies that individuals have discretion to perform their main operations in their own way, subject only to minimal collegial controls.'

The collegial model has been adopted by most universities. Authority of expertise is widespread within these institutions of scholarship and research. Glatter (1984, p. 23) describes universities as 'bottom-heavy institutions' and the nature of management should reflect this wide distribution of knowledge and competence. 'Any organisation which depends on high-level professional skills operates most efficiently if there is a substantial measure of collegiality in its management procedures' (Williams and Blackstone, 1983, p. 94).

The collegial model is most evident within the extensive committee system. Decisions on a whole range of academic and resource allocation issues take place within a labyrinth of committees rather than being the prerogative of the vice-chancellor. Issues are generally resolved by agreement or compromise rather than by voting or dissent: 'The members of a college take their own collective decisions, which have an authority legitimised by consensus, or at least compromise, amongst those to whom they apply' (Williams and Blackstone, 1983, p. 94). Collegial approaches may have originated within higher education but in many universities democracy is compromised by a limited franchise. Certain institutions give full voting rights to all academic staff and some representation to students and perhaps also non-academic staff. Elsewhere membership of senate and the key committees is the preserve of senior staff.

This restricted franchise serves to limit the extent to which universities can be regarded as collegial and many might be regarded as elitist rather than democratic:

> The . . . main shortcoming of consensual democracy relates to the criteria by which citizenship should be defined. Among what precise group of more or less equal citizens should consensus be obtained in this kind of democratic system? . . . Democracy is thus, in our view, a term which should be applied

with much greater care than is customary in discussions of university government if, indeed, it should be applied at all.
(Moodie and Eustace, 1974, pp. 223–4).

There is a dichotomy in universities and colleges between academic policy, which is generally the responsibility of the collegial senate or academic board, and resource management which is usually the preserve of the vice-chancellor and heads of faculty. The committee system fits the collegial model while the powers accorded directly to senior managers suggest one of the formal models. Kogan (1984, p. 28) points to the risk of conflict between the democratic and hierarchical aspects of higher education management:

> The tensions created by the two principles are present throughout the range of institutions. While the senate or academic board may have formal power over academic matters, these are also indirectly affected by the governing body by its power to allocate between different desirable academic ends. The head of the institution may be the servant of the senate or academic board when taking the chair, but is simultaneously accountable to the governing body for running the institution.

The rapid growth of higher education in the 1990s may have made it more difficult for the collegial aspects of universities to maintain their previous significance in the decision-making process. Middlehurst and Elton (1992, p. 261) argue that collegiality is threatened by the increased emphasis on competition:

> [Universities] have not only survived the 1980s, but in certain ways have prospered . . . by becoming more managerial . . . There is no doubt that in the short run this has worked, but we have quite serious doubts concerning the long term, particularly as one of the effects . . . has been a considerable loss in collegiality across the higher education system, with the resulting loss of a sense of ownership and shared professional responsibility for the operation of the institution.

The desire to maintain staff participation in decision-making may conflict with the pressure to become increasingly accountable to external funding and quality control bodies. This tension between participation and accountability is also evident in schools as we shall see later in this chapter.

## Collegial models in secondary schools

The introduction of collegial approaches in secondary schools has been slower, less complete and more piecemeal than in higher education. The tradition of all powerful heads, with authority over staff and accountability to external bodies, has stifled several attempts to develop participative modes of management. The formal position is that heads alone are responsible for the organization and management of schools. This consideration has acted as a brake on some heads who wish to share their power and as a convenient justification for those reluctant to do so.

An early example of a collegial model in operation was seen at Countesthorpe college in Leicestershire in the 1970s. The main policy-making body was the 'moot' which was open to all staff and students. It met every six weeks and all other decision-making bodies were responsible to it. The main standing committee held office for one quarter of the year and comprised one quarter of the staff with student representation. All meetings were advertised and open. Proposals could emanate from any group or individual. The former principal, John Watts, outlines the main collegial features at Countesthorpe:

> The major policy decisions that have shaped the curriculum and discipline of the school have been made by the consensus of the staff. Increasingly, students have contributed to this consensus, and in some cases parents and governors have participated. I accepted the headship in 1972 because I found the policies and the means of determining them attractive.
>
> (Watts, 1976, pp. 130–1)

The Countesthorpe approach incorporated all the central elements of collegial models, including acknowledgement of teachers' authority of expertise and the emphasis on consensual decision-making by all the staff with student input. This example also illustrates the normative nature of collegiality because Watts regarded the approach as 'attractive'.

## Churchfields High School

One school that has made significant progress towards collegial management in the 1980s and 1990s is Churchfields High School in West Bromwich. The headteacher, Edwin Smith, is committed to collegiality and he introduced several participative elements at Churchfields (Smith, 1991; Bush, 1993).

### The management structure

Since 1988 Churchfields has been developing a management structure to facilitate substantial involvement in decision-making. The school has 57 staff and so it has adopted representative collegiality. The central body is the Professional Policy and Planning (PPP) committee which comprises 13 staff. Two are elected by the whole staff and 2 by each of 3 subordinate groups, responsible for curriculum, pastoral and community matters. These 8 elected members are joined on PPP by the 5 members of the Central (formerly senior) Management Team: the headteacher, the curriculum director, the pastoral director, the community director and the bursar.

In addition to meetings of PPP and its three subordinate groups, there are also regular meetings of the whole staff, the faculties and house teams, governing body committees and parental groups. This is an elaborate structure which gives ample opportunity for staff and others to participate in school management.

### Management process

Most policy decisions are taken within the committee structure. The head claims that it is a participative process but other staff have different perceptions:

> 'Decision making is predominantly participative; not consultative but participative which for me is a more deep kind of involvement of staff. We have a

lot of committees, we have a lot of opportunities . . . for staff to take initiatives and generate issues' (head).

'Decisions are made at this school by the headmaster and his senior management team . . . [who] get their *information* from sub-committees which are co-ordinated by PPP' (head of department).

'I would like to think that major decisions were made by PPP but that isn't always the case. It depends on the urgency with which the decision has to be made. It also depends on quite how strongly various members of CMT might feel about the decision' (deputy head).

(Bush 1993, p. 37)

This last comment by a member of the Central Management Team suggests a conditional collegiality where some decisions are made through the participative process but senior staff retain a veto which may be used if unacceptable proposals emerge from the committee structure.

### The role of the head
Heads may appear to have reduced authority in an overtly collegial school like Churchfields. However, Edwin Smith retains significant influence for three main reasons:

- The head has an important role in determining what is to be discussed through his power over agenda-setting, a device usually associated with political models (see Chapter 5).
- He may feel so strongly about certain issues that staff recognise that his view is going to prevail: 'We went through processes where . . . we had consultation and we talked about it but whether we agreed or not we knew it was going to be implemented' (teacher).
- The requirement for heads to be accountable to governors and to external groups makes it difficult for them to go against their personal judgement. As one deputy stresses, 'the buck stops with the head'.

(Bush, 1993, pp. 37–9)

### The advantages of collegiality at Churchfields
There are three main advantages of collegiality. Firstly, there is ample evidence that teachers wish to participate more fully in the management of their schools (Davies 1983). The Churchfields system provides this opportunity: 'The really positive point is that I feel I can participate. Other members of my department can participate through me or indeed can go along and take part themselves. Everybody has a voice' (head of department, quoted by Bush, 1993, p. 39).

Secondly, the quality of decision-making is likely to be better where teaching staff participate in the process. Heads do not have a monopoly of wisdom or vision and the involvement of other staff increases the quotient of experience and expertise brought to bear on problems.

Finally, the participation of teaching staff is important because they usually have the responsibility for implementing changes in policy. Effective implementation is much more likely if teachers feel that they 'own' the decisions: 'I think we get better decisions . . . I also think we get staff who feel that they have a part in those decisions . . . they actually understand what the decision mean . . . the staff are more likely to want them to work' (headteacher, quoted by Bush, 1993, p. 39)

## The disadvantages of collegiality at Churchfields

While staff appreciate the advantages of collegiality they are also very conscious about the disadvantages. There appear to be four main problems:

1. The process is rather *slow* because decisions may take a long time to move through the elaborate committee system. A new staff structure took nearly a year to finalise because the proposals were subject to change and referred back to all relevant groups.
2. There are problems of communication amongst the groups and individuals involved in the process. One head of department says that 'people don't know what is going on at any one moment'.
3. The layout of the Churchfields campus, with many buildings spread across a large site, leads to teachers spending breaks in one of the many faculty staff rooms. This facilitates subunit collaboration but limits whole-school collegiality to formal set-piece events, a development which is consistent with 'contrived collegiality' (Hargreaves, 1994).
4. The need to hold meetings at the end of the teaching day affects staff motivation and the quality of decision-making. 'To be making decisions at half past three when perhaps you are not at your sharpest is not really the best way to do things . . . Participating in that many meetings in the twilight zone is very hard' (head of department quoted in Bush, 1993, pp. 39–40).

Churchfields has several collegial features. Staff have ample formal representation within the decision-making structure and decisions are usually reached by consensus. Despite his good intentions, the head recognizes that the school is not yet collegial. 'What is happening at Churchfields appears to be evolution towards collegiality, not yet collegiality itself. The evolutionary path is not linear; there are blind alleys and retreats, but the overall direction is towards collegiality' (Smith, 1991).

## Collegial models in primary schools

Collegiality has become established during the 1980s and 1990s as the most appropriate way to manage primary schools. It is now the normative model of good practice in this phase of education. Its main features are probably the following:

- Staff working groups determine proposals for decision by the whole staff.
- The working groups are led by curriculum co-ordinators or consultants.
- The co-ordinators progressively acquire expertise in their specialist area, drawing on external expertise.
- The co-ordinators work alongside class teachers to demonstrate ideas in practice.
- The teachers operate in a climate in which constructive scrutiny of practice is expected.

(Campbell, 1985, pp. 152–3)

Little (1990, pp. 177–80) describes how collegiality operates in practice and identifies the following elements of a collegial approach:

- Teachers talk about teaching.
- There is shared planning and preparation.
- The presence of observers in classrooms is common.
- There is mutual training and development.

The model outlined by Campbell (1985) and Little (1990) appears to depend on shared professional values leading to the development of trust and a willingness to give and receive criticism in order to enhance practice. It is a demanding approach that requires commitment from staff if it is to become an effective vehicle for beneficial change. It is also an elusive model to operate even where staff are committed to the concept.

## St Meryl Primary School

Gill Batterbee, the headteacher of St Meryl primary school, near Watford, offered to participate in research conducted by the author (Bush, 1993) because of her commitment to collegial approaches. The school has many collegial features but, as with Churchfields, there are certain difficulties in implementing this approach.

### Staff meetings
Meetings of the whole staff are held each Monday during directed time. All staff may raise items for discussion but the 'big' issues tend to be raised by Gill and her deputy. A significant feature of meetings is discussion about aspects of the curriculum led by the appropriate subject co-ordinator. Staff say that they 'generally reach consensus' at these meetings but Gill concedes that she is sometimes given the final say: 'There are sometimes occasions when you can't reach agreement . . . there are times when people say this is one for you . . . do you want to give a final decision?' (Bush, 1993, p. 27).

### The role of the head
Gill stresses that she wants staff, parents and children to feel 'ownership' of the school: 'St Meryl is not my school. It belongs to all of us' (Bush, 1993, p. 28). Staff refer to Gill's willingness to encourage teacher involvement in decision-making but also point out that she has clear views of her own which she communicates to staff. There may be tension between these two positions: 'Gill wants decision-making to be a "genuinely shared activity" but occasionally she will say that "something has to be done", because of the pressure of external accountability or because her own professional judgement is at odds with the staff view' (Bush, 1993, p. 28).

### The role of subject co-ordinators
At St Meryl, the subject co-ordinator has a low-key role. In the critical relationship between co-ordinator and class teacher, the initiative rests with the latter. Co-ordinators wait for an approach from colleagues and are not proactive in presenting ideas to class teachers. There is little shared teaching, as Gill

points out: 'I would love to say that we could have subject co-ordinators working alongside staff on a very regular basis but we don't have the finance and the time to allow that to happen' (Bush, 1993, p. 29).

### The nature of collegiality at St Meryl
St Meryl school appears to have several collegial features:

- Staff spend time discussing their teaching, both on formal occasions and during breaks.
- Subject co-ordinators make their expertise available to colleagues.
- Staff say that decisions are usually made by consensus.

However, the implementation of collegiality is subject to certain limitations:

- Gill may back her own judgement rather than staff opinion.
- There are limited opportunities for co-ordinators to work alongside class teachers.

(Bush, 1993, pp. 32–3).

There is a clear commitment to participative decision-making at St Meryl as the deputy head stresses: 'Ownership is important. If we were going to move anywhere we had to have people contributing and contributing actively' (Bush, 1993, p. 33). It is evident, however, that St Meryl operates a restricted form of collegiality, as Gill suggests: 'I think gradually we are moving more towards a collegiate system of operation in St. Meryl. I don't know whether we will ever become 100 per cent collegiate. I don't actually believe it's possible' (Bush, 1993, p. 33). The St Meryl case illustrates the view that collegiality is desirable but very difficult to operate in practice. Like the end of the rainbow, it is always just out of reach.

## Collegial models: goals, structure, environment and leadership

### *Goals*

Collegial models assume that members of an organization agree on its *goals*. There is a belief that staff have a shared view of the purposes of the institution. Agreement on aims is perhaps the central element in all participative approaches to school and college management. Livingstone (1974, p. 22) outlines the functions of institutional objectives:

> First of all, goals provide a general guide to activity. A member of an organisation who is aware of the organisation's goal is better able to make his activities relevant to achieving it. Secondly, goals serve as a source of legitimacy. Activities can be justified if they can be shown to further achievement of the goals. Thirdly, they are a means of measuring success. . . . An organisation is effective if it achieves its objectives.

Campbell and Southworth (1993, p. 72) emphasize the need for staff to 'purpose the same' and quote from their research in primary schools: 'Teachers felt that it was important that they should have compatible ideals, agree the same aims and share the same purpose . . . "If you are aiming for a whole-school . . .

then everybody has got to agree about aims and purposes".' The significance of
agreed goals as a basis for school policies and activities is stressed by Watts
(1976, pp. 133–4) in his discussion of Countesthorpe college:

> the participatory system depends upon an initial agreement of aims . . .
> Countesthorpe was made possible by the first head's clear announcement of
> intention which enabled him to recruit a staff who wanted to work in that
> way. With head and staff agreed on basics, any conflicts can be resolved by
> open discussion with reference to them, provided all parties learn to tolerate
> conflict, use it to identify issues and make compromises in order to reach
> consensus.

There is a clear indication here that agreement on goals, central to the ethos of
collegial models, is likely to be achieved only under certain conditions. One
circumstance, identified by Watts (1976), is where staff have been chosen by
the head and possess a common educational philosophy. At Wroxham primary
school, Potters Bar, staff appointments were critical elements in the development of shared aims:

> Most of the staff have been appointed since [the head's] arrival. She ex-
> pounds aspects of her philosophy in the job description for new posts. [One
> teacher] believes that she was appointed 'because I share this philosophy'.
> . . . [The head] is 'confident that new staff accept and endorse the aims'. She
> is perhaps less certain about the views of longer serving teachers.
>
> (Bush, 1988, p. 35)

In universities and colleges, and perhaps also in secondary schools, the
various academic disciplines often have rather different ideas about the central purpose of their institutions. In these circumstances, as Baldridge *et al.*
(1978, pp. 20–1) demonstrate, agreement on aims may be achieved only by
obfuscation: 'Most organisations know what they are doing. . . . By contrast,
colleges and universities have vague, ambiguous goals. . . . As long as goals
are left ambiguous and abstract, people agree; as soon as they are concretely
specified and put into operation, disagreement arises.' The acknowledgement
of possible conflict over the goals of educational institutions threatens one of
the central planks of collegial theory. The belief that staff can always reach
agreement over institutional purposes and policies lies at the heart of all
participative approaches. Recognition of goal conflict serves to limit the
validity of collegial models.

## Organizational structure

Collegial models share with formal approaches the view that organisational
*structure* is an objective fact which has a clear meaning for all members of the
institution. The major difference concerns the relationships between different
elements of the structure. Formal models present structures as vertical or
hierarchical with decisions being made by leaders and then passed down the
structure. Subordinates are accountable to superiors for the satisfactory performance of their duties. In contrast, collegial models assume structures to be
lateral or horizontal with participants having an equal right to determine
policy and influence decisions.

In education, collegial approaches are often manifested through systems of committees, which may be elaborate in the larger and more complex institutions. The decision-making process inside committees is thought to be egalitarian with influence dependent more on specific expertise than an official position. The assumption is that decisions are reached by consensus or compromise rather than acquiescence to the views of the head or principal.

In schools, *ad hoc* working parties may be more effective than standing committees. At Wroxham, there were several working parties that were regarded as effective in curriculum development, as the deputy head suggests: 'Staff meetings are not so good for curriculum development. It is more productive to promote informal discussion in the staff room. Smaller working parties work better with keen staff building up a document and presenting it to the whole staff' (Bush, 1988, p. 40). The Pensnett comprehensive school in Dudley also developed a system of working parties that were charged with reviewing issues and preparing recommendations. Final decisions were taken by senior staff and governors. This is not really a collegial approach but it does represent a shift along the continuum towards collaborative working:

> The . . . working parties represent a commitment to consultative approaches on the part of both the leadership and the staff at the Pensnett. It is not a truly democratic framework but the teachers appear to be generally satisfied with the opportunity to participate even if final decisions rest with senior management.
>
> (Bush, 1988, p. 38)

## The external environment

There are several difficulties in assessing the nature of relationships between the organization and its *external environment*. Collegial models characterize decision-making as a participative process with all members of the institution having an equal opportunity to influence policy and action. However, where decisions emerge from an often complex committee system, it is no easy task to establish who is responsible for organizational policy. Noble and Pym (1970, pp. 435–6) point to some of the elusive qualities of decision-making by committee:

> The most striking feature of the organisation to the newcomer or outsider seeking some response from it is the receding locus of power. In complex organisations in the spheres of education, industry, administration or commerce, this Kafkaesque experience is very common; wherever or at whatever level one applies to the organisation, the 'real' decisions always seem to be taken somewhere else.

The ambiguity of the decision-making process within collegial organizations creates a particular problem in terms of accountability to external bodies. The head or principal is invariably held responsible for the policies of the school or college. The assumptions of the formal models are in line with these expectations. Leaders are thought to determine or strongly influence decisions and are accountable to external bodies for these policies.

Collegial models do not fit comfortably with these formal accountability assumptions. Are heads expected to justify school policies determined within a participatory framework even where they do not enjoy their personal support? Or is the reality that collegial policy-making is limited by the head's responsibility to external agencies? Heads must agree with, or at minimum acquiesce in, decisions made in committee if they are not to be placed in a very difficult position. The former Cambridgeshire College of Arts and Technology illustrates the delicacy of such relationships:

> [The principal] . . . sees that his own credibility depends on his being able to 'carry' the academic board most of the time. If there were strong disagreements between his view and that of the academic board, he recognises that he would need to go to the governors and report in his capacity as chairman of the academic board and, differently, as principal: he recognises that this might result in a vote of no confidence by the academic board and appreciates that very few principals would be likely to survive this.
>
> (Bush and Goulding, 1984, p. 18)

Collegial models tend to overlook the possibility of conflict between internal participative processes and external accountability. The often bland assumption that issues can be resolved by consensus leads to the comfortable conclusion that heads are always in agreement with decisions and experience no difficulty in explaining them to external bodies. In practice, it may be that the head's accountability leads to a substantially modified version of collegiality in most schools and colleges. There is also the risk of tension for the principal who is caught between the conflicting demands of participation and accountability.

> Collegial methods may be difficult to sustain in view of the requirement that heads and principals remain accountable to the governing bodies which appoint them. While participation represents the internal aspect of collegiality, accountability may be thought of as the external dimension. Leaders may be sandwiched between these very different pressures. Ultimately they have to explain decisions to outside bodies and this creates difficulties when policies do not enjoy their personal support.
>
> (Bush, 1993, p. 12)

## Leadership

In collegial models the style of *leadership* both influences, and is influenced by, the nature of the decision-making process. Because policy is determined within a participative framework, the head or principal is expected to adopt strategies which acknowledge that issues may emerge from different parts of the organization and be resolved in a complex interactive process. Heroic models of leadership are inappropriate when influence and power are widely distributed within the institution:

> The collegial leader is at most a 'first among equals' in an academic organisation supposedly run by professional experts . . . The basic idea of the collegial leader is less to command than to listen, less to lead than to gather expert judgements, less to manage than to facilitate, less to order than to persuade and negotiate . . . the collegial leader is not so much a star standing alone as the developer of consensus among the professionals who must share the burden of the decision.
>
> (Baldridge *et al.*, 1978, p. 45)

Collegial theorists tend to ascribe the following qualities to leaders in schools and colleges:

1. They are responsive to the needs and wishes of their professional colleagues. Heads and principals acknowledge the expertise and skill of the teachers and seek to harness these assets for the benefit of the pupils and students. Invariably they have been appointed to leadership posts after a long period as successful practitioners. Their experience makes them 'sensitive to the informal codes of professional practice which govern expectations for relations among teachers and between teachers and head' (Coulson, 1985, p. 86).
2. Collegial heads seek to create formal and informal opportunities for the testing and elaboration of policy initiatives. This is done to encourage innovation and to maximize the acceptability of school decisions. As Brown (1983, p. 224) suggests in relation to primary schools: 'the headteacher who perceives his role as being that of a democrat . . . ensures that school organisation facilitates frequent staff discussion and co-ordination in order that decisions are made as a collective art'.
3. Collegial models emphasize the authority of expertise rather than official authority. It follows that authority in professional organizations such as schools or colleges resides as much with the staff as with the head. Instead of exerting authority over subordinates, the leader seeks to influence the decisions and actions of professional colleagues. The head also allows and encourages heads of department and curriculum co-ordinators to become co-leaders. The following passage develops this point in relation to primary schools: '[Collegial] leadership draws much of its justification from the authority of expertise of professional staff. The process of subject co-ordination reinforces this authority and establishes a cadre of specialists who are able to influence decisions by virtue of their accumulated knowledge of their subjects' (Bush, 1988, p. 42).

In collegial models, then, the head or principal is typified as the facilitator of an essentially participative process. Their credibility with their colleagues depends on providing leadership to staff and external stakeholders while valuing the contributions of specialist teachers: 'The picture of a "good" headteacher which emerged from the teachers' comments on a "whole school" was of a person to whom they could talk and with whom they could discuss, who did not dictate, who was effectively a part of the staff group and whose philosophy was clear and shared by colleagues' (Campbell and Southworth, 1993, p. 75). Heads and principals retain a pivotal role in the management of the institution and can exercise considerable influence over its direction as long as they retain the confidence and support of their professional colleagues. For Handy (1977, p. 186), this is the essential difference between formal approaches and collegial leadership, which depends on consent:

> The distinction between the organisation of consent and the traditional hierarchical organisation is that authority in the former is granted by those below whereas in the hierarchical state authority is conferred by those above. Your official role in the organisation of consent gives you little effective power – that is only won by the consent of those you seek to manage.

Nor does this consent, once given, hold good for all time or for all circumstances. It needs constant ratification.

This focus on consent is similar to the concept of 'transformational leadership' discussed by Caldwell and Spinks (1992, pp. 49–50). They argue that this mode of leadership is essential for autonomous schools: 'Transformational leaders succeed in gaining the commitment of followers to such a degree that . . . higher levels of accomplishment become virtually a moral imperative. In our view a powerful capacity for transformational leadership is required for the successful transition to a system of self-managing schools.'

## Collegiality and gender

The trend towards collegial management has been particularly noticeable in primary schools and most of the relevant literature refers to this sector. There may be several reasons for this disparity, including the fact that primary schools are generally small enough for 'whole-school' collegiality and have simple, unstratified structures. It may also be influenced by gender. Women invariably form the majority in primary schools and some have an all-female staff. There is also a much higher proportion of women leaders in primary schools than in secondary schools or colleges.

Al-Khalifa (1989, p. 89) claims that women adopt different management styles from men with a much greater emphasis on collaboration, co-operation and other 'feminine' behaviours. These styles, which are compatible with collegiality, are contrasted with 'masculine' aspects of management: 'Women managers pinpoint aspects of management practice which they find dysfunctional – namely aggressive competitive behaviours, an emphasis on control rather than negotiation and collaboration, and the pursuit of competition rather than shared problem-solving.'

Nias, Southworth and Yeomans (1989, pp. 70–1) discuss the applicability of a gender perspective to the collegial culture prevalent in many primary schools but conclude on the basis of their research that this view is 'simplistic':

> It could be argued that the 'culture of collaboration', with its emphasis on concern for the individual and on cohesion, its legitimation of emotionality, its validation of control both by peers and by the head, its denial of competition, is a 'woman's culture' . . . [but] to argue that a collaborative culture is gender-specific is simplistic.

Nias, Southworth and Yeomans (1989) refer to examples of successful collaborative behaviour involving both women and men. However, Coleman (1994) presents evidence that women managers in education tend to be more democratic than men, demonstrating qualities of warmth, empathy and co-operation. This issue requires further research before conclusions can be drawn with confidence.

## Limitations of collegial models

Collegial models have become increasingly popular in the literature on educational management and in official pronouncements about school development.

Their advocates believe that participative approaches represent the most appropriate means of conducting affairs in educational institutions. However, critics of collegial models point to a number of flaws which serve to limit their validity in schools and colleges. There are eight significant weaknesses of collegial perspectives.

1. Collegial models are so strongly *normative* that they tend to obscure rather than portray reality. Precepts about the most appropriate ways of managing educational institutions mingle with descriptions of behaviour. While collegiality is increasingly advocated, the evidence of its presence in schools and colleges tends to be sketchy and incomplete. Baldridge *et al.* (1978, p. 33) present a powerful critique of collegial models in higher education which may also apply to schools:

   > The collegial literature often confuses *descriptive* and *normative* enterprises. Are the writers saying that the university *is* a collegium or that it *ought* to be a collegium? Frequently, the discussions of collegium are more a lament for paradise lost than a description of present reality. Indeed, the collegial idea of round table decision making does not accurately reflect the actual processes in most institutions.

2. Collegial approaches to decision-making tend to be *slow and cumbersome*. When policy proposals require the approval of a series of committees, the process is often tortuous and time consuming. The participative ethic requires that a decision should be made by agreement where possible rather than by resorting to a voting process. The attempts to achieve consensus may lead to procedural delays such as a reference back to the sponsoring committee, or to consultation with other committees, individuals or external agencies. Participants may have to endure many lengthy meetings before issues are resolved. This requires patience and a considerable investment of time, as we noted earlier in respect of Churchfields High school. Hellawell (1991, p. 335) concludes that lack of time could be a serious constraint in primary schools: 'My own experience of collegial structures in higher education is that they are extremely time-consuming and they certainly demand a level of meetings that primary school personnel could only fulfil by using considerable time outside the school teaching hours.' The sheer length of the process may be a major factor in the relatively limited adoption of collegial approaches in schools. Most staff are engaged in classroom activities for much or all of the day. Meetings tend to be held after school when staff are tired and unprepared for a protracted attempt to achieve consensus on aspects of school policy.

3. A fundamental assumption of democratic models is that decisions are reached by *consensus*. It is believed that the outcome of debate should be agreement based on the shared values of participants. In practice, though, committee members have their own views and there is no guarantee of unanimity on outcomes. In addition, participants often represent constituencies within the school or college. Individuals may be members of committees as representatives of the English department or the science faculty. Inevitably these sectional interests have a significant influence on committees' processes. The participatory framework may become the focal point

for disagreement between factions. Baldridge *et al.* (1978, pp. 33–4) argue that democratic models greatly underestimate the significance of conflict within education:

> The collegial model . . . fails to deal adequately with the problem of *conflict* . . . [it] neglects the prolonged battles that precede consensus and the fact that the consensus actually represents the prevalence of one group over another. Collegial proponents are correct in declaring that simple bureaucratic rule making is not the essence of decision making, but in making this point they take the equally indefensible position that major decisions are reached primarily by consensus.

4. Collegial models have to be evaluated in relation to the special features of educational institutions. The participative aspects of decision-making exist alongside the structural and bureaucratic components of schools and colleges. Often there is tension between these rather different modes of management. The participative element rests on the authority of expertise possessed by professional staff but this rarely trumps the positional authority of official leaders. As Lortie (1969, p. 30) suggests, 'it seems unlikely that collegial ties play a major part in reducing the potency of hierarchical authority'.

5. Collegial approaches to school and college decision-making may be difficult to sustain in view of the requirement that heads and principals remain accountable to the governing body and to various external groups. Participation represents the internal dimension of democracy. *Accountability* may be thought of as the external aspect of democracy. Governors and external groups seek explanations of policy and invariably turn to the head or principal for answers to their questions. Heads may experience considerable difficulty in defending policies which have emerged from a collegial process but do not enjoy their personal support. Churchfields head Edwin Smith deals with this dilemma by suggesting that the collegial process itself is more important than the decisions resulting from that process:

> The headteacher works on the principle that if he thinks a decision is 'wrong' but there is consensus in favour of it, it is more likely to be made to work successfully than the decision he would have favoured. It is a matter of commitment to a decision by those who will have to make it work. The accountability is for successful implementation of policies, rather than for the policies themselves.
>
> (Smith, 1991).

While this statement represents a strong commitment to collegiality, it underestimates the accountability pressures and the impact they have on the extent and nature of collegiality in schools and colleges. In practice, the leader's accountability means that there cannot be more than a conditional democracy in education.

6. The effectiveness of a collegial system depends in part on the attitudes of staff. If they actively support participation then it may succeed. If they display apathy or hostility, it seems certain to fail. Hellawell (1991, p. 334) refers to the experience of one primary head who sought to introduce collegial approaches:

I have worked very hard over the last few years, as the number of staff has grown, to build up a really collegial style of management with a lot of staff input into decisions that affect the school and they are saying that they don't like this. They would like an autocracy. They would like to be told what to do.

Campbell (1985) and Wallace (1989) argue that teachers may not welcome collegiality because they are disinclined to accept any authority intermediate between themselves and the head. This has serious implications for the role of the curriculum co-ordinator: 'Potential tension is . . . embedded in the relationship between the roles of curriculum consultant and class-teacher. Many teachers expect a high degree of autonomy over the delivery of the curriculum in their classrooms, yet their professional judgement may conflict with that of the consultant' (Wallace, 1989, p. 187). This attitude may well account for the tentative way in which the co-ordinator role has been implemented in St. Meryl as in many other primary schools.

7. Collegial processes in schools depend even more on the attitudes of heads than on the support of teachers. In colleges, the academic board provides a legitimate forum for the involvement of staff in decision-making and principals have to recognize and work with this alternative power source. In schools, participative machinery can be established only with the support of the head, who has the legal authority to manage the school. Wise heads take account of the views of their staff but this is a consultative process and not collegiality. Hoyle (1986, p. 91) concludes that its dependence on the head's support limits the validity of the collegiality model:'Collegiality is not inherent in the system but is a function of leadership style whereby teachers are given the opportunity to participate in the decision-making process by benevolent heads rather than as of right.'

## Contrived collegiality

Hargreaves (1994) makes a more fundamental criticism of collegiality, arguing that it is being espoused or 'contrived' by official groups in order to secure the implementation of national policy in England and Wales and elsewhere. He claims that genuine collegiality is spontaneous, voluntary, unpredictable, informal and geared to development. Contrived collegiality, in contrast, has the following contradictory features:

- Administratively regulated rather than spontaneous.
- Compulsory rather than discretionary.
- Geared to the implementation of the mandates of government or the headteacher.
- Fixed in time and place.
- Designed to have predictable outcomes.

(Hargreaves, 1994, pp. 195–6).

Within the post-Education Reform Act context in England and Wales, this analysis is persuasive. These dimensions of 'collegiality' support his analysis:

- Collegiality receives official support (Campbell, 1985).

- The National Curriculum largely prescribes content and assessment.
- The concept of 'directed time' enables heads to prescribe participation in the decision-making process.

These elements do not necessarily eliminate the informal and spontaneous aspects of collegiality but they do lend support to Hargreaves' (1994) analysis.

## Conclusion: is collegiality an unattainable ideal?

Collegial models are highly normative and idealistic. Their advocates believe that participative approaches represent the most appropriate means of managing educational institutions. Teachers exhibit that authority of expertise which justifies their involvement in the decision-making process. In addition, they are able to exercise sufficient discretion in the classroom to ensure that innovation depends on their co-operation. Collegial theorists argue that active support for change is more likely to be forthcoming where teachers have been able to contribute to the process of policy formulation.

Collegial models contribute several important concepts to the theory of educational management. Participative approaches are a necessary antidote to the rigid hierarchical assumptions of the formal models. However, collegial perspectives provide an incomplete portrayal of management in education. They underestimate the official authority of the head and present bland assumptions of consensus which often cannot be substantiated. Hoyle (1986, p. 100) argues that bureaucratic and political realities mean that collegiality does not exist in schools: 'In the absence of a true collegium, a situation which the existing law and external expectations preclude, the head either carries a fully-participating staff or fails to do so thus creating a situation of direct conflict.' This view may be too pessimistic but it remains true that those who aspire to collegiality often find that it cannot be implemented effectively. Little (1990, p. 187), following substantial research in the United States, concludes that collegiality 'turns out to be rare'.

A generation ago almost all schools and colleges could have been categorized as formal. In the 1990s, many are developing collegial frameworks. There is a discernible trend towards collegiality. It is uneven but it is tangible. Despite Hargreaves' (1994) justifiable criticisms of 'contrived collegiality', the advantages of participation in professional organizations remain persuasive. Collegiality is an elusive ideal but it is likely to become an increasingly significant model within the theory of educational management.

## References

Al-Khalifa, E. (1989) Management by halves: women teachers and school management, in H. De Lyon and F. Migniuolo (eds.) *Women Teachers: Issues and Experiences*, Open University Press, Milton Keynes.

Baldridge, J. V., Curtis, D. V., Ecker, G. and Riley, G. L. (1978) *Policy Making and Effective Leadership*, Jossey Bass, San Francisco.

Becher, T. and Kogan, M. (1992) *Process and Structure in Higher Education*, Second Edition, Routledge, London.

Brown, C. M. (1983) Curriculum management in the junior school, *School Organisation*, Vol. 3, no. 3, pp. 221-8.

Bush, T. (1988), *Action and Theory in School Management, E325 Managing Schools*, The Open University, Milton Keynes.

Bush, T. (1993) *Exploring Collegiality: Theory. Process and Structure, E326 Managing Schools: Challenge and Response*, The Open University, Milton Keynes.

Bush, T. and Goulding, S. (1984) *Cambridgeshire College of Arts and Technology: Facing the Cuts, E 324 Management In Post Compulsory Education, Block 3, Part 4*, Open University Press, Milton Keynes.

Caldwell, B. and Spinks, J. (1992), *Leading the Self-Managing School*, The Falmer Press, London.

Campbell, R. J. (1985) *Developing the Primary Curriculum*, Holt, Rinehart and Winston, London.

Campbell, P. and Southworth, P. (1993) Rethinking collegiality: teachers' views, in N. Bennett, M. Crawford and C. Riches (eds.) *Managing Change in Education: Individual and Organizational Perspectives*, Paul Chapman Publishing, London.

Coleman, M. (1994) Women in educational management, in T. Bush and J. West-Burnham (eds.) *The Principles of Educational Management*, Longman, Harlow.

Coulson, A. (1985) *The Managerial Behaviour of Primary School Heads*, Collected Original Resources in Education, Carfax Publishing Company, Abingdon.

Davies, B. (1983) Head of department involvement in decisions, *Education Management and Administration*, Vol. 11, no. 3, pp. 173-6.

Glatter, R. (1984) *Managing for Change, E324 Management in Post Compulsory Education, Block 6*, Open University Press, Milton Keynes.

Handy, C. B. (1977) The organisations of consent, in D. W. Piper and R. Glatter (eds.) *The Changing University*, NFER-Nelson, Windsor.

Hargreaves, A. (1994) *Changing Teachers, Changing Times: Teachers' Work and Culture in the Postmodern Age*, Cassell, London.

Hellawell. D. (1991) The changing role of the head in the primary school in England, *School Organisation*, Vol. 11, no. 3, pp. 321-37.

Hoyle, E. (1986) *The Politics of School Management*, Hodder and Stoughton, Sevenoaks.

Kogan, M. (1984) *Models and Structures, E324 Management in Post Compulsory Education*, Open University Press, Milton Keynes.

Little, J. (1990) Teachers as colleagues, in A. Lieberman (ed.) *Schools as Collaborative Cultures: Creating the Future Now*, The Falmer Press, Basingstoke.

Livingstone, H. (1974) *The University: An Organisational Analysis*, Blackie, Glasgow.

Lortie, D. C. (1969) The balance of control and autonomy in elementary school teaching, in A. Etzioni (ed.) *The Semi-Professions and Their Organisation*, Free Press, a division of Macmillan Inc., New York.

Middlehurst, R. and Elton, L. (1992) Leadership and management in higher education, *Studies in Higher Education*, Vol. 17, no. 3, pp. 251-64.

Moodie, G. C. and Eustace, R. (1974) *Power and Authority in British Universities*, George Allan and Unwin, London.

Nias, J., Southworth, G. and Yeomans, R. (1989) *Staff Relationships in the Primary School*, Cassell, London.

Noble, T. and Pym, B. (1970) Collegial authority and the receding locus of power, *British Journal of Sociology*, Vol. 21, pp. 431-45.

Richman, B. M. and Farmer, R. N. (1974) *Leadership, Goals and Power in Higher Education*, Jossey Bass, San Francisco.

Smith, E. (1991) Collegiality in practice: a case study of a Midlands comprehensive school. Paper presented at the Open University residential school, Nottingham, April.

Wallace, M. (1989) Towards a collegiate approach to curriculum management in primary and middle schools, in M. Preedy (ed.) *Approaches to Curriculum Management*, Open University Press, Milton Keynes.

Watts, J. (1976) Sharing it out: the role of the head in participatory government, in R. S. Peters (ed.) *The Role of the Head*, Routledge and Kegan Paul, London.

Williams, K. (1989) The case for democratic management in schools, *Irish Educational Studies*, Vol. 8, no. 2, pp. 73–86.

Williams, G. and Blackstone, T. (1983) *Response to Adversity*, Society for Research into Higher Education, Guildford.

# 5

# Political Models

## Central features of political models

Political models embrace those theories which characterize decision-making as a bargaining process. They assume that organizations are political arenas whose members engage in political activity in pursuit of their interests. Analysis focuses on the distribution of power and influence in organizations and on the bargaining and negotiation between interest groups. Conflict is regarded as endemic within organizations and management is directed towards the regulation of political behaviour. The definition suggested below incorporates the main elements of these approaches:

> Political models assume that in organizations policy and decisions emerge through a process of negotiation and bargaining. Interest groups develop and form alliances in pursuit of particular policy objectives. Conflict is viewed as a natural phenomenon and power accrues to dominant coalitions rather than being the preserve of formal leaders.

Politics tend to be regarded as the concern of central and local government and to be associated strongly with the political parties who compete for our votes at general, local and European elections. It is useful to loosen this close identity between government and politics before seeking to apply political metaphors to educational institutions.

National and local politics strongly influence the context within which schools and colleges operate. Central government determines the broad character of the educational system and this is inevitably underpinned by the political views of the majority party. The 1988 Education Reform Act, for example, with its emphasis on self-managing schools competing for clients, has its genesis in the Conservative Party's philosophy that market principles serve to improve performance.

Local politics have become less influential since the 1988 Act which allocated many former LEA responsibilities to central government or to the educational institutions. However, LEAs retain the power to determine the funding position of most schools through its control over the LMS formula. The elements of the formula, and their weighting, are the product of the political judgements of the majority party, within the limitations laid down in the legislation.

While national and local government determine the broad framework for education, political models apply to schools, colleges and other organizations just as much as they relate to political parties:

> I take schools, in common with virtually all other social organizations, to be riven with actual or potential conflict between members; to be poorly co-ordinated; to be ideologically diverse. I take it to be essential that if we are to understand the nature of schools as organizations, we must achieve some understanding of these conflicts. (Ball, 1987, p. 19)

The relevance of political models to educational institutions is acknowledged by both academics and practitioners. Within education these perspectives are often referred to as 'micropolitics'. Glatter (1982, p. 16) claims that micropolitics is 'an essential perspective':

> The language of power, coalitions, arenas, contests, bargaining, negotiations, interests, ambiguity and so on seems very helpful in distinguishing rhetoric from reality . . . in drawing attention to the different purposes which different individuals, groups and institutions have and the various ways they set about attaining them. . . . the approaches which may be broadly termed the micropolitical perspective are essential to an understanding of educational administration and management.

Baldridge (1971, pp. 19–20) conducted research in universities in the USA and concluded that the political model, rather than the formal or collegial perspectives, best captured the realities of life in higher education:

> When we look at the complex and dynamic processes that explode on the modern campus today, we see neither the rigid, formal aspects of bureaucracy nor the calm consensus-directed elements of an academic collegium. On the contrary . . . [interest groups] emerge . . . These groups articulate their interests in many different ways, bringing pressure on the decision-making process from any number of angles . . . Power and influence, once articulated, go through a complex process until policies are shaped, reshaped and forged out of the competing claims of multiple groups.

Political models may be just as valid for schools and further education as they are for universities.

Political models have the following major features:

1. They tend to focus on *group activity* rather than the institution as a whole. The emphasis is on the basic unit (Becher and Kogan, 1992) not the school or college level. Interaction between groups is at the heart of political approaches whereas formal and collegial models stress the institutional level: 'The basic unit of traditional political analysis is the sub group . . . the basic unit of an apolitical perspective is the total system' (Bacharach and Lawler, 1980)

   In education much of the political analysis centres on the influence of academic departments. Marland (1982, pp. 122–3) refers to 'the traditional political power of heads of departments' and deprecates their sectional approach to school policy-making:

The status and self esteem of heads of departments seems to be increased the narrower the view and decreased if they develop a broader vision. For instance members of a subject department will sharply criticise their head of department if she or he does not push unremittingly for the self interest of the department. Thus, the good team leader is felt by the team as one who demands adamantly, ostentatiously, and consistently for more teachers, more space, more money, more equipment, more rooms, more pupils, smaller groups, and, above all, more of the pupils' time.

Ball (1987, p. 221) refers to 'baronial politics' and discusses the nature of conflict between the leaders of subgroups: 'In the middle ages the conflicts between English barons were essentially concerned with two matters: wealth and power. In the school the concerns and interests of academic and pastoral barons are fundamentally the same: allocations from the budget . . . and influence over school policies.' Pursaill (1976) refers to the political role of heads of department in further education in the 1970s. He says that college structures tend to be 'feudal' with heads of department exercising 'baronial rights'. While college organization tends to be more diverse in the 1990s (see Chapter 3, p.32), middle managers still compete for resources and power through an essentially political process.

2. Political models are concerned with *interests* and *interest groups*. Individuals are thought to have a variety of interests which they pursue within the organization. Hoyle (1986, p. 128) distinguishes between personal and professional interests: 'Professional interests . . . centre on commitments to a particular curriculum, syllabus, mode of pupil grouping, teaching method, etc. . . . professional interests become part of the micropolitical process according to the strategies used to further them. Personal interests focus on such issues as status, promotion and working conditions' Hoyle (1982, p. 89) points to the development of interest groups as a principal means of seeking and achieving individual aims:

> Interests are pursued by individuals but frequently they are most effectively pursued in collaboration with others who share a common concern. Some of these may have the qualities of a group in that they are relatively enduring and have a degree of cohesion, but others . . . will be looser associations of individuals who collaborate only infrequently when a common interest comes to the fore.

The more permanent interest groups, such as departments, are cohesive because of shared values and beliefs. The individuals within such groups have common attitudes towards many of the central issues in schools and colleges. However, there are differences in goals and values *between* interest groups, leading to fragmentation rather than organizational unity. On particular issues, groups may form alliances to press for policies which reflect their joint interests. These coalitions may well be temporary, disbanding when certain objectives have been achieved, while the interest groups themselves often have enduring significance.

3. Political models stress the prevalence of *conflict* in organizations. Interest groups pursue their independent objectives which may contrast sharply with the aims of other subunits within the institution and lead to conflict between them: 'The leader, as the one responsible for the overall goals of

the organisation, must be aware of the differing values and interests which are at the root of conflict within organisations' (Wilkinson, 1987, p. 60). An important feature of political perspectives is the view that conflict is a normal feature of organizations. Collegial models have a strong harmony bias and the possibility of disagreement is ignored or assumed away. In contrast, Baldridge *et al.* (1978, p. 35) regard conflict in educational institutions as both inevitable and welcome: 'In a fragmented, dynamic social system, conflict is natural and not necessarily a symptom of breakdown in the academic community. In fact, conflict is a significant factor in promoting healthy organisational change.' It is important to distinguish between constructive and destructive forms of conflict; it may be a positive rather than a negative element within organizations.

4. Political models assume that the *goals* of organizations are unstable, ambiguous and contested. Individuals, interest groups and coalitions have their own purposes and act towards their achievement. Goals may be disputed and then become a significant element in the conflict between groups. Certain subunits succeed in establishing their goals as the objectives of the institution while other interests seek to supplant the official purposes with their own objectives. Cyert (1975, p. 28) discusses the nature of disagreement between interest groups and the institution.

> Within any organisation conflicts tend to arise between the goals of subunits and the overall goals of the total organisation. These conflicts frequently are based on a professional goal and that subunit desires to achieve the resources that the organisational management is prepared to allocate toward the achievement of that goal.

Interest groups are likely to promote their objectives in a variety of ways until they are supported by the policy-makers. This does not necessarily end the conflict because the endorsement of one set of purposes tends to be at the expense of other goals, whose proponents may continue to lobby for their own ideas. Disagreement over goals is a continuing feature of the policy process in organizations.

5. In political arenas decisions emerge after a complex process of *bargaining and negotiation*. Formal models assume that decisions follow a rational process. Options are evaluated in terms of the objectives of the organization and the most appropriate alternative is selected.

Policy-making in political settings is a more uncertain business. Interests are promoted in committees and at numerous unofficial encounters between participants. Policies cannot easily be judged in terms of the goals of the institution because these are subject to the same process of internal debate and subsequent change. The objectives are a moving target, as Bolman and Deal (1984, pp. 109–10) suggest:

> Organisational goals and decisions emerge from ongoing processes of bargaining, negotiation, and jockeying for position among individuals and groups . . . [Each group] wants to have an impact on organisational decisions and attempts to do so by participating in a multistage process that includes articulation of interests, efforts to get those interests translated into institutional policy, resolution of conflicting forces into an accepted policy, and implementation of decisions that have been attained.

The emphasis on the several stages of decision-making is significant because it multiplies the opportunities available to interest groups to exert influence on the policy process. Decisions on a subject at one forum do not necessarily resolve the issue because the unsuccessful groups are likely to pursue the matter whenever opportunities arise or can be engineered.

6. The concept of *power* is central to all political theories. The outcomes of the complex decision-making process are likely to be determined according to the relative power of the individuals and interest groups involved in the debate. These participants mobilize resources of power which are deployed in support of their interests and have a significant impact on policy outcomes, as Mangham (1979, p. 17) demonstrates: 'what underpins the decision and produces the action . . . is the direct result of the power and the skill of the proponents and opponents of all the action in question. Decisions and actions within organisations may be seen as the consequence of the pulling and hauling that is politics.' The connections between interest groups, conflict and power are examined by Morgan (1986). He regards these elements as the central processes of political behaviour:

> We can analyze organizational politics in a systematic way by focusing on relations between interests, conflict and power. Organizational politics arise when people think differently and want to act differently. This diversity creates a tension that must be resolved through political means . . . Divergent interests give rise to conflicts, visible and invisible, that are resolved or perpetuated by various kinds of power play.
>
> (Morgan, 1986, p. 148).

The nature and sources of power in education are examined on pages 79–82.

## Baldridge's Political Model

Several of the ideas discussed in the previous section are brought together in the political model developed by Baldridge (1971). The author considers the formation of interest groups and discusses the ways in which policies emerge from the kaleidoscope of conflicting pressures (see Figure 5.1). Baldridge postulates five stages in the policy process:

1. A *social structure* is a configuration of social groups with basically different lifestyles and political interests. These differences often lead to conflict, for what is in the interest of one group may damage another. The social structure, with its fragmented groups, divergent goal aspiration, and conflicting claims on the decision makers, is the setting for political behaviour. Many conflicts have their roots in the complexity of the social structure and in the complex goals and values held by divergent groups.

2. *Interest articulation* is the process by which interests are advanced. Groups with conflicting values and goals must translate them into effective influence if they are to obtain favourable action by legislative bodies. How does a powerful group exert its pressure, what threats or promises can it make, and how does it translate its desires into political capital? There are many forms of interest articulation and it assumes a multitude of shapes.

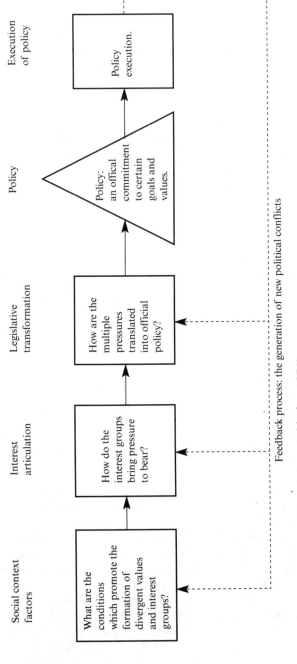

**Figure 5.1** A political model (from Baldridge, 1971)

3. The *legislative stage* is the process by which articulated interests are translated into policies. Legislative bodies respond to pressures, transforming the conflict into politically feasible policy. In the process many claims are played off against one another, negotiations are undertaken, compromises are forged, and rewards are divided. Committees meet, commissions report, negotiators bargain, and powerful people 'haggle' about the eventual policy.

4. The *formulation of policy* is the end result of the legislative stage. The articulated interests have gone through conflict and compromise stages and the final legislative action is taken. The policy is the official climax to the conflict and represents an authoritative, binding decision to commit the organization to one set of possible alternative actions, to one set of goals and values.

5. Finally the *execution of policy* occurs. The conflict comes to a climax, the battle is at least officially over, and the resulting policy is turned over to the bureaucrats for routine execution. This may not be the end of the matter, however, for two things are likely to happen. First, the major losers in the conflict may take up their arms again for a new round of interest articulation. Second, the execution of policy inevitably causes a *feedback cycle*, in which the policy generates new tensions, new vested interests, and a new cycle of political conflict.

(Baldridge, 1971, pp. 23–4).

Baldridge (1971, p. 24) summarizes his model as follows: 'A complex social structure generates multiple pressures, many forms of power and pressure impinge on the decision makers, a legislative stage translates these pressures into policy, and a policy execution phase finally generates feedback in the form of new conflicts.' Perhaps the most significant aspect of the Baldridge model is that it is essentially iterative. The policy-making process is rarely straightforward. Rather, it is capable of breakdown at any stage as opposing interests coalesce to defeat proposals and seek to substitute their own plans. This leads to the feedback processes which inevitably follow the breakdown of particular proposals. Ultimately the success or failure of interest groups in promoting their objectives depends on the resources of power which they are able to mobilize.

## Sources of power in education

Power may be regarded as the ability to determine the behaviour of others or to decide the outcome of conflict. Where there is disagreement it is likely to be resolved according to the relative resources of power available to the participants. 'Power is the medium through which conflicts of interest are ultimately resolved. Power influences who gets what, when, and how' (Morgan 1986, p. 158).

There are many sources of power but in broad terms a distinction can be made between authority and influence. Authority is legitimate power which is vested in leaders within formal organizations. Authority involves a legal right to make decisions which may be supported by sanctions. Influence represents an ability to affect outcomes and depends on personal characteristics and expertise. Bacharach and Lawler (1980, p. 44) identify seven distinctions between authority and influence:

1. Authority is the static, structural aspect of power in organizations; influence is the dynamic, tactical element.
2. Authority is the formal aspect of power; influence is the informal aspect.
3. Authority refers to the formally sanctioned right to make final decisions; influence is not sanctioned by the organization and is, therefore, not a matter of organizational rights.
4. Authority implies involuntary submission by subordinates; influence implies voluntary submission and does not necessarily entail a superior-subordinate relationship.
5. Authority flows downward, and it is unidirectional; influence is multi-directional and can flow upward, downward, or horizontally.
6. The source of authority is solely structural; the source of influence may be personal characteristics, expertise, or opportunity.
7. Authority is circumscribed, that is, the domain, scope, and legitimacy of the power are specifically and clearly delimited; influence is uncircumscribed, that is, its domain, scope, and legitimacy are typically ambiguous.

Hoyle (1982, p. 90) points to the ways in which these two aspects of power operate within educational institutions:

> Influence differs from authority in having a number of sources in the organization, in being embedded in the actual relationships between groups rather than located in an abstract legal source, and is not fixed but is variable and operates through bargaining, manipulation, exchange and so forth. The head teacher in Britain has a high degree of authority; but his [sic] exercise of that authority is increasingly modified as teachers' sources of influence . . increase and thus involves the head in a greater degree of exchange and bargaining behaviour.

There are six significant forms of power relevant to schools and colleges:

1. *Positional power*    a major source of power in any organization is that accruing to individuals who hold an *official position* in the institution. Formal positions confer authority on their holders, who have a recognized right to make decisions or to play a key role in the policy-making process. In schools the head is regarded as the legitimate leader and possesses legal authority which is inevitably a key determinant of school policy. Other staff who hold senior posts may also exercise positional power. These may include deputy heads, heads of department and pastoral leaders. Chairs of governing bodies may also exert positional power within self-managing schools and colleges. In a hierarchy the more highly placed individuals exert the greater authority:

> The first and most obvious source of power in an organization is formal authority, a form of legitimized power that is respected and acknowledged by those with whom one interacts . . . legitimacy is a form of social approval that is essential for stabilizing power relations, and arises when people recognize that a person has a right to rule some area of human life (Morgan, 1986, p. 159)

2. *Authority of expertise* in professional organizations there is a significant reservoir of power available to those who possess appropriate *expertise*. Schools and colleges employ many staff who have specialist knowledge of aspects of the curriculum. The music specialist, for example, is regarded as the expert and principals may be cautious in substituting their own judgements for those of their heads of department in curricular matters. In certain circumstances there may be conflict between formal leaders and experts but the outcome is by no means certain: 'Expert power relates to the use of knowledge and expertise as a means of legitimizing what one wishes to do. "The expert" often carries an aura of authority and power that can add considerable weight to a decision that rests in the balance' (Morgan, 1986, p. 169).

3. *Personal power* individuals who are charismatic or possess verbal skills or certain other characteristics may be able to exercise *personal power*. Staff who are able to influence behaviour or decisions by virtue of personal abilities or qualities are often thought to possess the attributes of charismatic leadership. These personal skills are independent of the power accruing to individuals by virtue of their position in the organization. In school staff rooms, for example, there are often individuals who command the respect of colleagues because of their perceived wisdom or insight. These teachers may become alternative leaders whose views are sought on the key issues. According to Bacharach and Lawler (1980), leadership is primarily a product of personal qualities rather than official position: 'Leadership encompasses the personal abilities and characteristics that key individuals have apart from their offices or other sources of power.' Personal power clearly depends on influence rather than authority.

4. *Control of rewards* power is likely to be possessed to a significant degree by individuals who have *control of rewards*. They are inevitably perceived as powerful by those who value such returns. In education, rewards may include promotion, good references and allocation to favoured classes or groups. Individuals who control or influence the allocation of these benefits may be able to determine the behaviour of teachers who seek one or more of the rewards. Typically the head or principal is the major arbiter of promotion and references although advice may be sought from heads of department or others who possess relevant knowledge or information. Classes may be allocated by heads of department. This form of power represents a means of control over aspiring teachers but may have little influence on those staff who choose to spurn these rewards. Control of rewards may be regarded as authority rather than influence where it emanates from the leader acting in an official capacity.

. *Coercive power* the mirror image of the control of rewards may be *coercive power*. This implies the ability to enforce compliance with a request or requirement. Coercion is backed by the threat of sanctions. Heads may exercise coercive power by threatening not to supply a good reference for external applications or warning about the prospects for internal promotion. In certain circumstances, coercion may be used in conjunction with the control of rewards to manipulate the behaviour of others. This 'carrot and stick' combination may have a powerful double effect on staff and may be a latent factor in all schools and colleges. In a hierarchy it is assumed that leaders have a right to seek the compliance of staff as long as the instructions are legitimate. In this sense coercive power may be regarded as authority rather than influence.

6. *Control of resources*   control of the *distribution of resources* may be an important source of power in educational institutions, particularly in self-managing schools and colleges. Decisions about the allocation of resources are likely to be among the most significant aspects of the policy process in schools and colleges. Resources include not only revenue and capital finance but also human and material resources such as staff and equipment. Control of these resources may give power over those people who wish to acquire them. There is often competition between interest groups for additional resources and success or failure in acquiring extra finance, staff and other resources is an indicator of the relative power of individuals and groups: 'If politics is regarded as conflict over whose preferences are to prevail in the determination of policy, then the budget records the outcomes of this struggle' (Wildavsky, 1968, p. 192).

Consideration of these six sources of power leads to the conclusion that heads and principals possess substantial resources of authority and influence. They have the capacity to determine many institutional decisions and to affect the behaviour of their colleagues. However, they do not have absolute power. Other leaders and staff also have power, arising principally from their personal qualities and expertise. Lay governors may also be powerful, particularly if they chair the governing body or one of its important committees. These other sources of power may counter-balance the head's positional authority and control of rewards.

## Political strategies in education

Educational leaders may adopt one or more political strategies in order to maintain or extend their control or to ensure a favoured outcome to a decision process. Using their significant resources of power, they are often able to ensure support for, or compliance with, their preferred position. Hoyle (1986, pp. 140–6) outlines some of the more significant strategies:

1. *Dividing and ruling*   this may involve heads arranging separate deals with individuals or departments, for example in respect of resource allocation.
2. *Co-optation*   this entails the involvement of those who support the leader or whose potential opposition has to be diverted. It may be used simply to involve a certain individual in the decision process or may be an attempt to manipulate the outcome.
3. *Displacement*   this occurs where the apparent issue is used to cloak the real purpose of the participant. A good example is where personal interests, such as status, are presented as 'professional'. This might occur where heads of department argue for more time for their subject.
4. *Controlling information*   information is an important source of power. Heads and principals are the main recipients of external information and may use this to influence decisions.

5. *Controlling meetings* leaders may be able to control the outcomes of meetings by using one or more of the following devices:

- 'rigging' agendas;
- 'losing' recommendations;
- 'nobbling' members of the group;
- invoking outside bodies;
- 'massaging' minutes.

## Exchange theory

Another political strategy is to engage in a process of 'exchange' with other members of the organization. Leaders, in particular, may seek to offer 'rewards' to other participants to secure compliance with their wishes but this approach is open to all those who have something to 'exchange'.

Exchange theory is closely linked to the concept of power, as Bacharach and Lawler (1980, p. 19) suggest:

> power is a central aspect of an exchange approach to social relationships, and dependence or independence constitutes the point of departure for analysing power. . . . Dependence is what makes exchange an integral part of any social relationship. Without dependence, there is no reason for an exchange, because parties can operate and obtain outcomes in total isolation.

Exchange theory is identified with the work of Blau (1964) and Homans (1958; 1974) who offer the following definitions:

> Social exchange . . . refers to the voluntary actions of individuals that are motivated by the returns they are expected to bring and typically do in fact bring from others.
>
> (Blau, 1964, p. 91)

> Social behaviour is an exchange of goods, material goods but also non-material ones, such as the symbols of approval or prestige. Persons that give much to others try to get much from them, and persons that get much from others are under pressure to give much to them. This process of influence tends to work out at equilibrium at this point in the exchanges.
>
> (Homans, 1958, p. 606)

The concept of exchange is a profitable way of examining relationships in education. Heads and principals possess authority arising from their positions as the formal leaders of their institutions. They also hold power in the form of key rewards such as promotion and references. However, the head requires the co-operation of staff to secure the effective management of the school. An exchange may secure benefits for both parties to the arrangement. Hoyle (1981) outlines the goods or rewards available to heads and teachers engaging in a process of exchange:

> Material resources.
> Promotion.
> Esteem for other staff.
> Autonomy for favoured teachers.
> Lax application of rules for certain teachers.

Hoyle (1981) points out that there is an imbalance between the bargaining resources of the head and of the teacher. The latter has fewer 'goods' to trade and these tend to be symbolic rather than material. Nevertheless, these may be important to the head:

- Esteem for the head.
- Support for the head's aims.
- Opinion leadership: influencing the staff to support the head.
- Conformity to rules laid down by the head.
- Reputation: enhancing the prestige of the school (and hence of the head) through examination or sporting success, etc.

(Hoyle, 1981, p. 17)

Exchanges may also occur between teachers in schools and colleges. For example one teacher may agree to support another's claim to additional resources on the understanding that the gesture is reciprocated, perhaps on a different occasion. This links back to the notion of alliances and coalitions discussed earlier (p. 75). Exchange theory is likely to be useful in understanding behaviour in many different situations in educational institutions.

## Political models: goals, structure, environment and leadership

### Goals

Political models differ from both the formal and collegial approaches in that they focus primarily on the *goals* of subunits, or looser groups of individuals, rather than the objectives of the institution itself. Ball (1987, p. 11) claims that the focus on organizational goals in much of the literature is a 'major distortion' and prefers to emphasize the goal diversity of organizations.

These models assume that groups advance their interests in the form of goals that are pursued vigorously within the institution. Mangham (1979, p. 16) claims that 'organisations may be said to consist of many groups and individuals, multiple coalitions and alliances and each acting so as to achieve its own set of goals and objectives'. The collegial assumption that there is agreement over the goals of the organization is challenged by political theorists who argue that there is no such consensus: 'An assumption of consensus . . . has extremely limited validity in almost all types of organizations' (Ball, 1987, p. 11).

Schools and colleges have multiple goals reflecting the various interest groups. These groups endeavour to promote their own objectives as the official purposes of the institution. Inevitably, the goals of the various groups sometimes conflict with one another because a focus on one objective may be at the expense of another: 'Goals may be inherently in conflict and . . . these conflicts will become manifest when the goals are given a specific form in terms of pedagogy or curriculum' (Hoyle, 1986, p. 58). The Pensnett school in Dudley experienced conflict over the relative importance of academic and pastoral goals. Heads of department emphasized examination successes and basic skills while pastoral leaders stressed the personal and social development of the child (Bush, 1988, p. 47).

As a result of this inter-group conflict, goals tend to be ambiguous, unstable and contested. Bolman and Deal (1984, p. 111) stress that organizational goals emerge from a process of bargaining and negotiation. 'Different individuals and groups have different objectives and resources, and each attempts to bargain with other members or coalitions in order to influence the goals and decision making of the system.' The capacity to secure institutional backing for group objectives depends crucially on the power of the interest group and the ability of its members to mobilize support from other subunits and institutional leaders. There is a continuing process of negotiation and alliance building to muster sufficient support for the group's policy objectives. Goals are unstable because alliances break down and new factors are introduced into the bargaining process. The extant objectives may be usurped by purposes advanced by new coalitions of interests.

Ultimately, goals become 'organizational' according to the resources of power that can be mobilised in their support. The purposes of the most powerful groups emerge as organizational goals. This occurred at The Pensnett school in the early 1980s when the power of department heads, and the support of the headteacher, led to the dominance of academic goals (Bush, 1988, p. 47).

## Organizational structure

Political models assume that *organizational structure* emerges from the process of bargaining and negotiation and may be subject to change as the interest groups jockey for position. Formal and collegial approaches present structure as a stable aspect of the organization while political theorists regard it as one of the uncertain and conflictual elements of the institution. The structure is developed not so much for organizational effectiveness, as formal theorists suggest, but rather to determine which interests are to be served by the organization:

> Organizational structure[s] . . . are often best understood as products and reflections of a struggle for political control . . . organizational structure is frequently used as a political instrument.
>
> (Morgan, 1986, pp. 162–3)

> So the groups agree on ways of dividing up power and resources, and those divisions are reflected in the design of the organisation.
>
> (Bolman and Deal, 1984, p. 141)

Schools and colleges provide many illustrations of structure being established or adapted following political activity. A management team drawn primarily from heads of department, for example, may be seen as a device to reinforce their baronial power.

Wilkinson (1987) shows how manipulation of the structure by a new head led to a redistribution of power within a secondary school. He abolished the posts of heads of humanities, science and modern languages and promoted teachers to head the relevant subjects within these former departments. He also demoted year heads by introducing heads of lower and middle school. These fundamental changes led to a diminution of formal power amongst staff hostile to the new leader. 'Almost overnight the headteacher had destroyed the most powerful coalition in the school. The newly promoted people would . . .

owe their allegiance to him . . . some would say that these are "improper" . . . tactics' (Wilkinson, 1987, p. 54).

Hoyle (1986) argues that schools are particularly prone to political activity because of their 'loosely-coupled' structure (see Chapter 7). The partial autonomy of teachers and their authority of expertise, together with the sectional interests of different subunits, leads to this structural looseness and the prevalence of 'micropolitics':

> The loosely-coupled structure of the school invites micropolitical activity since, although the head has a high degree of authority and responsibility, the relative autonomy of teachers and the norms of the teaching profession, serve to limit the pervasiveness and scope of this power . . . Thus heads frequently have recourse to micropolitical strategies in order to have their way. But teachers, too, are not without their micropolitical resources.
>
> (Hoyle, 1986, p. 171)

The different parts of the structure, once established, are portrayed as potential battlegrounds where the interest groups engage in combat to secure the supremacy of their policy objectives. The various committees and more informal groups are settings for the continuing conflict between participants. Ebbutt and Brown's (1978, p. 8) research in colleges illustrates this point:

> Each of the staff interviewed at colleges A, B and C was asked whether in his opinion the academic board was an independent body making decisions in a coherent way with a mind of its own and on its own initiative, or whether it was more a forum in which competing interests within the college sought to get their own way through bargaining and adjustment. The answers given tended towards the latter view, which was also the author's impression from the documents recording the consultative process.

At Wroxham primary school in the 1980s the fortnightly staff meeting became the setting for conflict about, ironically, the frequency of staff meetings. The head wanted to move to weekly meetings but this was resisted by a faction of long-serving staff. The argument was eventually resolved by a compromise. The fortnightly meeting was retained but it was supplemented by staff working parties set up to prepare curriculum documents (Bush, 1988). This issue is less likely to occur following the introduction of 'directed time' but it serves to illustrate how elements of school structure may become the setting for political conflict.

## The external environment

Political models emphasize the significance of *external influences* on internal decision-making. The political process includes inputs from outside bodies and individuals which are often mediated by the internal participants. Sergiovanni (1984, p. 6) explains the nature of the interaction between educational institutions and external groups:

> The political perspective is concerned with the dynamic interplay of the organisation with forces in its external environment. Schools and universities, for example, are viewed as open rather than closed systems, as integral parts of a larger environment not as bounded entities isolated from the environment. They receive inputs, process them, and return outputs to the

environment. Inputs are presumed to be diverse and output demands often conflicting. As a result there is constant interplay between school and environment.

In this respect political approaches are similar to the open systems theories considered in Chapter 3. The major difference concerns the ways in which external pressures are imported into school or college decision-making. In formal models it is assumed that outside influences are transmitted through heads or principals whose knowledge of the external environment reinforces their official authority. The leaders' interpretation of these pressures may then be a significant element in the decision-making process.

In political models it is thought that external factors may be introduced by interest groups as well as by heads and principals. In further education, for example, staff whose courses are threatened by low enrolments may cite evidence from employers who value the threatened courses. These environmental pressures mingle with the internal factors and add to the complexity and ambiguity of decision-making. Baldridge *et al.* (1978, p. 36) stress the significance of outside interests: 'External interest groups exert a great deal of influence over the policy making process. And external pressures and formal control by outside agencies . . . are powerful shapers of internal governance processes.' The various groups which have an interest in educational institutions tend to have rather different motivations for their involvement. Official bodies may be concerned about educational standards, or 'value for money', and may exert their authority through the head or principal. Unofficial groups usually pursue sectional interests. Employers may want the school to instil particular skills while parents understandably focus on the progress of their own children. These pressures may be transmitted through the staff most involved with their interests rather than via the leader.

The management of the external environment is a significant issue for leaders and participants in political organizations. Control of the 'boundary' between schools and their environments is an important source of influence in the debate about policies and resources. Knowledge about the opinions and predilections of clients and interest groups confers power: 'By monitoring and controlling boundary transactions people are able to build up considerable power . . . Most people in leadership positions at all levels of an organization can engage in this kind of boundary management in a way that contributes to their power' (Morgan, 1986, p. 169).

## Leadership

There are two central facets of *leadership* within political arenas. In the first place the head or principal is a key participant in the process of bargaining and negotiation. Leaders have their own values, interests and policy objectives which they seek to advance as appropriate at meetings of committees and in informal settings. Heads have substantial reserves of power which they may deploy in support of their personal and institutional goals. Leaders also have a significant impact on the nature of the internal decision-making process and can exercise a controlling influence on the proceedings of committees. At one college examined by Ebbutt and Brown (1978) 'there was general agreement that the principal manipulated the agenda items, and even the minutes to some extent, to suit himself'. At a new secondary school studied by Wilkinson (1987, pp. 50–1), the head adopted several political strategies to control the apparently participative decision process:

- Determining the agenda.
- Controlling the contents of discussion documents.
- Promoting teachers who shared his values.

The headteacher of Pensnett school in Dudley used his control of rewards in a different way. He favoured mixed ability teaching and promoted this approach by allocating extra resources from a 'curriculum development fund' to departments seeking to move to mixed ability groups (Bush, 1988, p. 52).

The second facet of leadership concerns heads' responsibility to sustain the viability of the organization and to develop the framework within which policies can be tested and, ultimately, receive the endorsement of the various interest groups. To achieve acceptable outcomes, leaders become mediators who attempt to build coalitions in support of policies. There is a recurring pattern of discussion with representatives of power blocks to secure a measure of agreement. This may involve concessions and compromises so that the more powerful groups achieve benefits in exchange for their support:

> Management can then be seen as a process of engaging in or regulating conflict, bargaining, power and exchange. Political models therefore emphasize the scope for managerial discretion in determining objectives. A prerequisite for effectiveness is that the purposes of powerful individuals or groups within the organisation are satisfactorily met.
>
> (Cuthbert, 1984, p. 53)

## The limitations of political models

Political models are primarily descriptive and analytical unlike most other theories which tend to be normative. The focus on interests, conflict between groups and power provides a valid and persuasive interpretation of the decision-making process in schools and colleges. Teachers and managers often recognize the applicability of political models in their own schools and colleges. However, these theories do have five major limitations:

1. Political models are immersed so strongly in the language of power, conflict and manipulation that they neglect other standard aspects of organizations. There is little attempt to discuss the various processes of management or any real acknowledgement that most organizations operate for much of the time according to routine bureaucratic procedures. The focus is heavily on policy formulation while the implementation of policy receives little attention. Political perspectives probably understate the significance of organizational structure as a constraint on the nature of political activity. The outcomes of bargaining and negotiation are endorsed, or may falter, within the formal authority structure of the school or college. Baldridge is widely recognized as the leading writer on the application of political models to

education but he acknowledges that modifications are required to accommodate certain aspects of the more formal approaches:

> Our original political model probably underestimated the impact of routine bureaucratic processes. Many decisions are made not in the heat of political controversy but because standard operating procedures dominate in most organizations. . . . the model downplayed long-term patterns of decision processes and neglected the way institutional structure shaped and channelled political efforts.
>
> (Baldridge *et al.*, 1978, pp. 42–3)

2. Political models stress the influence of interest groups on decision-making and give little attention to the institutional level. The assumption is that organizations are fragmented into groups which pursue their own independent goals. These subunits compete to establish the supremacy of their policy objectives and to secure their endorsement within the institution. This aspect of political models may be inappropriate for most primary schools which do not have a departmental structure or any other apparatus which could become a focal point for political activity. The institutional level may be the centre of attention for staff in these schools, invalidating the political model's emphasis on interest group fragmentation.

3. In political models there is too much emphasis on conflict and a neglect of the possibility of professional collaboration leading to agreed outcomes. The assumption that staff are continually engaged in a calculated pursuit of their own interests underestimates the capacity of teachers to work in harmony with colleagues for the benefit of their pupils and students. The focus on power as the determinant of outcomes may not be wholly appropriate for a cerebral profession such as teaching. In many situations, staff may well be engaged in genuine debate about the best outcomes for the school rather than evaluating every issue in terms of personal and group advantage: 'The [political] frame is normatively cynical and pessimistic. It overstates the inevitability of conflict and understates the potential for effectiveness and collaboration' (Bolman and Deal, 1984).

4. Political models are regarded primarily as descriptive or explanatory theories. Their advocates claim that these approaches are realistic portrayals of the decision-making process in schools and colleges. Unlike collegial models, these theories are not intended to be normative or idealistic. There is no suggestion that teachers *should* pursue their own self-interest, simply an assessment, based on observation, that their behaviour is consistent with a political perspective. Nevertheless, the less attractive aspects of political models may make them unacceptable to many educationists: 'The amorality that often characterises political perspectives raises questions of values. To what extent does the political perspective, even as it purports to be simply a description of reality, ratify and sanctify some of the least humane and most unsavoury aspects of human systems?' (Bolman and Deal, 1984, p. 146).

5. Political models offer valid insights into the operation of schools and colleges but it is often difficult to discern what constitutes political behaviour and what may be typical bureaucratic or collegial activity. The interpreta-

tion of group processes as either 'collegial' or 'political' is particularly difficult. Campbell and Southworth's (1993, p. 77) research in primary schools illustrates this point: 'It would be simplistic to say the heads in the collaborative schools controlled what happened there but they certainly exerted a great deal of influence and they sometimes used their power directly . . . the heads . . . revealed a micropolitical dimension to collegiality.' A more cynical interpretation of this duality is that leaders seek to present decisions as collegial while simultaneously working to ensure the supremacy of their own views:

> The head is political. He [*sic*] does things collegially to be seen to be doing so outside. He pretends things are not his decisions but those of the working party. They are all his decisions but he doesn't like to be seen making them. If he doesn't like what they are doing, the working party would soon die the death. But you can't criticise a decision since he claims that it was not his decision.
>
> (Bailey, 1982, p. 104).

## Conclusion: are political models valid?

Political models provide rich descriptions and persuasive analysis of events and behaviour in schools and colleges. The explicit recognition of interests as prime motivators for action is valid. The acceptance that competing interests may lead to conflict, and that differential power ultimately determines the outcome, is a persuasive element in the analysis of educational institutions: 'The model of interests, conflict, and power . . . provides a practical and systematic means of understanding the relationship between politics and organization and emphasises the key role of power in determining political outcomes' (Morgan, 1986, p. 195). For many teachers the emphasis on power as the major determinant of policy outcomes is convincing and fits their day-to-day experience better than any other model. Bolman and Deal (1984, p. 144) argue that political models capture several of the essential features of institutions: 'The political frame presents the only realistic portrayal of organisations . . . The political frame says that power and politics are central to organisations and cannot be swept under the rug. The perspective represents an important antidote to the antiseptic rationality sometimes present in structural analysis.'

Despite their limitations, political models have much to offer in developing an appreciation of the nature of management in schools and colleges. Political theorists rightly draw attention to the significance of groups as a potent influence on policy formulation. The emphasis on conflict may be overdrawn but it is valuable as a counterbalance to the idealistic harmony bias of collegial models. The view that disagreement is likely to be resolved ultimately by the relative power of participants is also a persuasive contribution to our understanding of educational institutions. Political models provide valuable insights into the operation of schools and colleges but, as Baldridge *et al.* (1978, pp. 43–4) demonstrate, they need to be considered alongside the formal and collegial models:

> This political model is not a substitute for the bureaucratic or collegial models of academic decision making. In a very real sense each of those

addresses a separate set of problems and they often provide complementary interpretations. The political model also has many strengths, however, and we offer it as a strong contender for interpreting academic governance.

# References

Bacharach, S. B. and Lawler, E. J. (1980) *Power and Politics in Organisations*, Jossey Bass, San Francisco.

Bailey, T. (1982) The question of legitimation: a response to Eric Hoyle, *Educational Management and Administration*, Vol. 10, no. 2, pp. 99–106.

Baldridge, J. V. (1971) *Power and Conflict in the University*, John Wiley, New York.

Baldridge, J. V., Curtis, D. V., Ecker, G. and Riley, G. L. (1978) *Policy Making and Effective Leadership*, Jossey Bass, San Francisco.

Ball, S. (1987) *The Micropolitics of the School: Towards a Theory of School Organization*, Methuen, London.

Becher, T. and Kogan, M. (1992) *Process and Structure in Higher Education*, Second Edition, Routledge, London.

Blau, P. M. (1964) *Exchange and Power in Social Life*, John Wiley, New York.

Bolman, L. G. and Deal, T. E. (1984) *Modern Approaches to Understanding and Managing Organisations*, Jossey Bass, San Francisco.

Bush, T. (1988) *Action and Theory in School Management*, E325 *Managing Schools*, Open University Press, Milton Keynes.

Campbell, P. and Southworth, G. (1993) Rethinking collegiality: teachers views, in N. Bennett, M. Crawford and C. Riches (eds.) *Managing Change in Education: Individual and Organizational Perspectives*, Paul Chapman Publishing, London.

Cuthbert, R. (1984) *The Management Process*, E324 *Management In Post Compulsory Education, Block 3, Part 2*, Open University Press, Milton Keynes.

Cyert, R. M. (1975) *The Management of Non Profit Organisations*, Lexington Books, Lexington, Massachusetts.

Ebbutt, K. and Brown, R. (1978) The structure of power in the F.E. college, *Journal of Further and Higher Education*, (NATFHE) Vol. 2, no. 3, pp. 3–17.

Glatter, R. (1982) The micropolitics of education: issues for training, *Educational Management and Administration*, Vol. 10, no. 2, pp. 160–5.

Homans, G. C. (1958) Social behaviour as exchange, *American Journal of Sociology*, Vol. 63, no. 6, pp. 597–606.

Homans, G. C. (1974) *Social Behaviour: Its Elementary Forms*, Harcourt Brace Jovanovich, New York.

Hoyle, E. (1981) *The Process of Management*, E323 *Management in the School, Block 3, Part 1*, Open University Press, Milton Keynes.

Hoyle, E. (1982) Micropolitics of educational organisations, *Educational Management and Administration*, Vol. 10, no. 2, pp. 87–98.

Hoyle, E. (1986) *The Politics of School Management*, Hodder and Stoughton, Sevenoaks.

Langham, I. (1979) *The Politics of Organisational Change*, Associated Business Press, Ludgate House, Fleet Street, London.

Marland, M. (1982) The politics of improvement in schools, *Educational Management and Administration*, Vol. 10, no. 2, pp. 119–34.

Morgan, G. (1986), *Images of Organization*, Sage, Newbury Park, California.

Pursaill, A. J. (1976) *Staff Development in Further Education at a Time of Crisis*, Coombe Lodge Reports, no. 9, pp. 277–85.

Sergiovanni, T. J. (1984) Cultural and competing perspectives in administrative theory and practice, in T. J. Sergiovanni and J. E. Corbally, *Leadership and Organisational Culture*, University of Illinois Press, Chicago.

Wildavsky, A. (1968) Budgeting as a political process, in D. Sills (ed.), *International Encyclopaedia of the Social Sciences*, Cromwell, Collier and MacMillan, New York.
Wilkinson, J. (1987) *The Micropolitical Dimensions of Leadership in Secondary Schools*, Sheffield City Polytechnic, Sheffield.

# 6

# Subjective Models

## Central features of subjective models

Subjective models incorporate those approaches which focus on individuals within organizations rather than the total institution or its subunits. The individual is placed at the centre of the organization. These perspectives suggest that each person has a subjective and selective perception of the organization. Events and situations have different meanings for the various participants in institutions. Organizations are portrayed as complex units which reflect the numerous meanings and perceptions of all the people within them. Organizations are social constructions in the sense that they emerge from the interaction of their participants. They are manifestations of the values and beliefs of individuals rather than the concrete realities presented in formal models. The definition suggested below captures the main element of these approaches:

> Subjective models assume that organizations are the creations of the people within them. Participants are thought to interpret situations in different ways and these individual perceptions are derived from their background and values. Organizations have different meanings for each of their members and exist only in the experience of those members.

Subjective models include phenomenological and interactive approaches. While these perspectives are not identical, they are sufficiently close to be treated together and, indeed, to be used interchangeably in much of the literature (Innes-Brown, 1993). Hoyle (1986, p. 10) defines phenomenology and explains its link with interactionism:

> [These] perspectives . . . share certain characteristics which constitute a radically different way of conceiving social reality . . . The phenomenological approach gives priority to people and their actions. The social world essentially consists of people interacting with each other, negotiating patterns of relationships and constructing a view of the world.

Subjective models became prominent in educational management as a result of the work of Thomas Greenfield in the 1970s and 1980s. Greenfield is concerned about several aspects of systems theory which he regards as the dominant model of educational organizations. He argues that systems theory is 'bad theory' and criticizes its focus on the institution as a concrete reality:

> Most theories of organisation grossly simplify the nature of the reality with which they deal. The drive to see the organisation as a single kind of entity with a life of its own apart from the perceptions and beliefs of those involved in it blinds us to its complexity and the variety of organisations people create around themselves.
>
> (Greenfield, 1973, p. 571)

Greenfield's criticism of conventional (largely bureaucratic) theory is even more trenchant in his 1986 article on 'the decline and fall of science in educational administration':

> We have a science of administration which can deal only with facts and which does so by eliminating from its consideration all human passion, weakness, strength, conviction, hope, will, pity, frailty, altruism, courage, vice and virtue . . . in its own impotence [it] is inward-looking, self-deluding, self-defeating, and unnecessarily boring.
>
> (Greenfield, 1986, p. 61)

Greenfield's work has had a significant impact on theory development in educational management, as Hodgkinson (1993, p. x) suggests: 'It is not possible to properly comprehend the contemporary discipline of educational administration without some familiarity and aquaintanceship with the thoughts of Thomas Barr Greenfield.' Greenfield is closely associated with the application of subjective theories to schools and colleges and much of the theory development has come from him, or from others stimulated or provoked by his work.

Subjective models have the following major features:

1. They tend to focus on the beliefs and perceptions of *individual* members of organizations rather than the institutional level or interest groups. While formal and collegial models stress the total institution and political models emphasize subgroups, the individual is at the heart of subjective or phenomenological theories: 'Phenomenology then seeks to understand as far as we can understand by putting the individual at the centre of the stage where . . . other approaches tend to see the individual as one of the collectivity to which the individual generally conforms (Bruce, 1977, pp. 115–16).

   Within schools and colleges, subjective theorists point to the different values and aspirations of individual teachers, support staff and pupils. They all experience the institution from different standpoints and interpret events and situations according to their own background and motivations. Ribbins *et al.* (1981, p. 170) argue that 'The school is not the same reality for all its teachers. Each teacher brings a perspective to the school, and to his place within it, which is to some extent unique. There are . . . as many realities as there are teachers.'

   The focus on individuals rather than the organization is a fundamental difference between subjective and formal models and creates what Hodgkinson (1993, p. xii) regards as an unbridgeable divide. 'In the tension between individual and organization . . . there is more than a mere dialectical conflict. There can also be a chasm, a Great Divide, an abyss. A fact can *never* entail a value, and an individual can *never* become a collective.'

2. Subjective models are concerned with the *meanings* placed on events by people within organizations. The focus is on the individual interpretation of behaviour rather than the situations and actions themselves. According to Greenfield (1975, p.83), 'Organisations are to be understood in terms of people's beliefs about their behaviour within them', rather than on the basis of external observations of that behaviour. It is assumed that individuals may have different interpretations of the same event, as Silverman (1970, p. 130) suggests: 'People assign meanings to situations and to the actions of others and react in terms of the interpretation suggested by these meanings . . . The same individual even may, at different times or in different situations, assign varying meanings to what appears to an observer to be the same act.'

In schools there may be differences of interpretation between the head and other staff who often derive divergent meanings from the same event. Hoyle (1981, p. 45) draws attention to one familiar example of such discrepancies:

> When a head talks about his school on public occasions teachers often remark that they do not recognise the place, and, because this view of reality is different from that of the head's they may assume that he is deliberately misleading. But a phenomenological view would hold that we have here *competing* realities, the head and the teachers see the world differently with each perspective having its own legitimacy.

This case illustrates the point that the school or college may be conceptualized differently by the various individuals and groups in the organization. These participants construct a reality out of their interests and any commonality of perspective arises from the fortuitous fact that their interests are held in common (Hoyle, 1986).

3. The different meanings placed on situations by the various participants are products of their *values, background and experience*. So the interpretation of events depends on the beliefs held by each member of the organization. Holmes (1986, p. 80) argues that it is 'bizarre' to develop a theory of educational administration outside a framework of values:

> The lack of consensus about the purpose of elementary and secondary schools makes it more important rather than less to have a clear framework of goals and values. The modern idea that schools can function in a value-free atmosphere brings the whole educational profession, and particularly administrators, into disrepute.

Greenfield (1979, p. 103) asserts that formal theories make the mistake of treating the meanings of leaders as if they were the objective realities of the organization:

> Life in organisations is filled with contending ideologies . . . Too frequently in the past, organisation and administrative theory has . . . taken sides in the ideological battles of social process and presented as 'theory' the views of a dominating set of values, the views of rulers, elites, and their administrators.

One possible outcome of the different meanings placed on events may be conflict between participants. Where there are 'competing systems of interpretation' (Silverman, 1970), subjective models may take on some of the characteristics of political theories. Where meanings coincide, individuals may come together in groups and engage in political behaviour in pursuit of objectives. Greenfield (1986, p. 72) relates conflict to differences in values: 'Conflict is endemic in organizations. It arises when different individuals or groups hold opposing values or when they must choose between accepted but incompatible values. Administrators represent values, but they also impose them.' In subjective models, then, conflict is regarded as the product of competing values. However, conflict is only one of several possible outcomes and should not be regarded as a norm. Rather the assumption is that meanings are highly personal, often subtle, and subject to the values and experience of participants.

4. Subjective models treat *structure* as a product of human interaction rather than something which is fixed or predetermined. The organization charts which are characteristic of formal models are regarded as fictions in that they cannot predict the behaviour of individuals. Subjective theorists reject the view that people have to conform to the structure of organizations.

> Most managers appear to be of the opinion that structure in organisations is pre-existent, that all organisations have a predetermined structure into which people must fit. This is not so. Structure is simply a description of what people do and how they relate; organisation structure is a grossly simplified description of jobs and relationships. . . . A structure cannot be imposed on an organisation, it can only derive from what people do.
>
> (Gray, 1982, p. 34)

Subjective approaches move the emphasis away from structure towards a consideration of behaviour and process. Individual behaviour is thought to reflect the personal qualities and aspirations of the participants rather than the formal roles they occupy. Greenfield (1980, p. 40) claims that the variable nature of human behaviour means that organizations are subject to change: 'There is no ultimate reality about organisations, only a state of constant flux. Organisations are at once both the products of action and its cause. We act out of past circumstances and drive towards those we intend for the future. Social realities are constantly created and re-shaped.'

Subjective theorists are particularly critical of those models which attribute 'human' characteristics to organizations or regard structure as something independent of its members. Silverman (1970, p. 134) comments on this tendency to 'reify' organizations: 'The existence of society depends upon it being continuously confirmed in the actions of its members. . . . We reify society if we regard it as having an existence which is separate from and above the actions of men [sic].'

This perspective on the relative significance of structure and behaviour has implications for the management of organizations. It suggests that more attention should be given to the theory and practice of staff motivation, and to other aspects of human resource management, and that rather less significance should be attached to issues of organizational structure.

5. Subjective approaches emphasize the significance of individual purposes and deny the existence of organizational *goals*. Greenfield (1973, p. 553)

asks 'What is an organisation that it can have such a thing as a goal'? The view that organizations are simply the product of the interaction of their members leads naturally to the assumption that individuals, and not organizations, have objectives. The formal model's portrayal of organizations as powerful goal-seeking entities is treated with disdain:

> In subjective theory, because organisations have no corporeal existence apart from the experience members have of them, there can be no 'objectives' for an organisation only objectives for individual members. Furthermore, the nature of organisations as associations of people means that they are at best means to an end; that is they serve purposes. The purposes, however, are individual purposes – whatever members require the organisation to do in order that something or other may be achieved.
>
> (Gray, 1982, p. 35)

## Applying the subjective model – Rivendell School

The essence of subjective models is the view that the individual participant is at the heart of organizations and should not be regarded as simply a cog within the institution. The meanings placed on events by staff, governors and students are thought to be central to our understanding of schools and colleges. Analysis of educational institutions thus requires a subjective dimension if a complete picture is to emerge. However, there are very few empirical studies of schools or colleges which have adopted a subjective or phenomenological perspective. One significant exception is the study of pastoral care at Rivendell school (Best *et al.*, 1979; 1983; Ribbins *et al.*, 1981).

In their two-year study of Rivendell, Best and his colleagues give explicit recognition to the value of subjective approaches while acknowledging the methodological difficulties they pose:

> We accept the force of the argument that to explain any social phenomenon it is necessary to establish the subjective meanings which relevant actors attach to the phenomenon, but it is difficult to see how one can establish *meanings* in any hard and fast way. Meanings are not directly observable in the world like physical objects are, and it would be folly indeed to imagine that imputing meanings to actors or situations was something the researcher could lightly undertake.
>
> (Best *et al.*, 1983, p. 58)

The researchers adopted several approaches to ascertain the meanings placed on events by staff at Rivendell. There were interviews with 59 of the 82 staff, supported by observation of teachers in various situations. Any discrepancies between the accounts of different staff, or inconsistencies between teachers' comments and their behaviour, were taken up at subsequent interviews: 'In this way, we were able to reach a position in which we are fairly confident of the validity of the interpretations we finally made' (Best *et al.*, 1983, pp. 61–2). The authors' interpretation of the stated views and behaviour of Rivendell's teachers depended on the context of the statement or action. The implication of the study is that staff may modify their opinions according to the occasion and the nature of the audience. This variation in the manifest positions of teachers makes it difficult to ascertain their real feelings about situations and events:

What a teacher *says* has to be interpreted in the light of the *context* in which he says it . . . Although at Rivendell many senior staff spoke warmly and supportively of the school's pastoral care arrangements at meetings of feeder school parents, this was not necessarily the case at other times. In the context of interviews and informal discussions with researchers, some of these teachers showed themselves capable of a criticism of the school's pastoral arrangements to which their statements in more public situations gave no clue.

(Ribbins *et al.*, 1981, pp. 162–3)

Best and his colleagues were concerned to test the 'conventional wisdom' that teachers have the interests of the children at the heart of their approach to pastoral care. Their hypothesis was that there may be significant differences between the public statements and the reality of pastoral care in schools. The authors' approach to this apparent contradiction was to focus on the subjective interpretations of staff rather than the official version of pastoral care policy.

In developing an analytical theory of the growth of institutional pastoral care, we have given great weight to the actors and their perceptions of the 'problem' to which pastoral care is intended to provide the solution. Their perceptions will . . . be influenced by their own interests . . . . The naive assumption that pastoral care systems deal only with the problems of the children pre-empts a consideration of the possibility that the creation of pastoral care systems and their posts of responsibility may have been a response to problems confronting teachers, headteachers, LEAs and educational administrators.

(Best *et al.*, 1979, pp. 36–8)

The authors identify a number of variables which may have contributed to the growth of pastoral care concepts and structures in schools. These include comprehensive reorganization, the raising of the school leaving age and the demands for an adequate career structure, particularly for non-graduates from former secondary modern schools. All those individuals with an interest in the school apply their own interpretations to events and these necessarily influence the development of pastoral care practice in schools.

The public statements about pastoral care at Rivendell reflect the conventional wisdom of a child-centred approach. Staff have an obvious interest in maintaining and enhancing the reputation of their school and official pastoral care policy has to be interpreted in that light:

Headteachers and senior staff have a vested interest in portraying their school as a 'caring' institution because their own public image, and therefore to some extent their *self*-image, depends in no small measure on the evaluation which the public at large make of the institution for which they are responsible. This is heightened when a school is in the position of Rivendell Comprehensive, battling constantly against what staff believed to be an unjustifiably poor reputation in the local community.

(Best *et al.*, 1983, p. 57

Examples of the discontinuity between the school's official policy and pastoral care practice occurred during the research period at Rivendell. Ribbins *et al* (1981, p. 166) record one significant incident which serves to highlight this contrast:

We once interviewed a fairly senior member of staff who spent some time telling us how much he cared for children and how the 'interests' of his pupils came first with him. At this point a lower school boy knocked, and without waiting for permission, entered the room. He was immediately subjected to a diatribe of impressive proportions and sent from the room to 'wait to be dealt with later'. Once the boy had left, the teacher took up his account exactly where he had left it before the interruption, but to two researchers who were now a good deal more sceptical than they had been a few minutes before.

The numerous perceptions which emerged from the many interviews and observations at Rivendell were classified by the authors into five perspectives on pastoral care:

- Child-centred.
- Pupil-centred.
- Discipline-centred.
- Administrator-centred.
- Subject-centred.

These perspectives represent clusters of the various interpretations of school policy suggested by the staff. The five approaches are illustrated by extracts from the researchers' field notes and interview transcripts.

The *child-centred* perspective focuses on the problems of the child as an individual. It centres on issues of personal happiness and adaptation and supports the conventional wisdom of the school as a caring environment for its pupils. One teacher gave the following example of a pastoral care problem which the authors classified as 'child-centred':

> I have a girl who was a battered baby . . . she is very much a 'loner'. She had a bowel problem as well which makes her unpopular with other children . . . every time she had a PE period she would run away. When I asked her why, all she would say was 'I hate this school'. I got some of the girls together and talked about how we needed to convince her that we liked her. The girls cooperated in this. Now she doesn't run away. . . . Now she thinks she likes the school.
>
> (Best *et al.*, 1983, p. 65)

In this case the teacher interpreted the situation as a problem of personal happiness and adaptation rather than as a disciplinary problem. The solution adopted by the teacher was essentially child-centred and involved an interpersonal strategy which appeared to be successful.

The *pupil-centred* perspective relates primarily to children in their academic roles as pupils. The pastoral provision in the school is evaluated in terms of its function as a facilitator of a pupil's academic performance, as one teacher's comment suggests: 'What you have to do is to try to get to a position where the child can do his [sic] best work . . . To get the best work you must care for the child' (Best *et al.* 1983, p. 68). Here the concern for pupils' welfare is mainly geared to the promotion of their learning rather than the personal happiness of the children as individuals.

The *discipline-centred* perspective focuses on problems of teachers' control in the classroom and the difficulties created by the failure of other staff to give them support. Here the school's pastoral care provision is perceived as a vehicle for the control of pupils. One form tutor, when asked about her role, responded in part by emphasizing the importance of discipline:

> There are school problems, for example, if they are in trouble with another teacher. If it comes to my attention I say 'I don't want children in my class to be in trouble'. If they get into trouble I tell them I will do something about it; that is, not only will the teacher punish them but I will punish them as well.
>
> (Best *et al.*, 1983, p. 71)

For certain teachers the pastoral care structure of the school was assessed in terms of discipline and control. Pastoral staff were there to be 'used' by teachers to resolve their problems of control. Rivendell has both a house system and a year structure and one tutor was asked to distinguish between the vertical and horizontal structures. His response fits the discipline-centred approach to pastoral care:

> As far as I can see, there is little in the way of distinguishing features between them. In individual cases the Head of House may be stronger than the Head of Year, so you go to the former. At least this arrangement gives you two bites at the cherry: if one doesn't pay off the other does.
>
> (Best *et al.*, 1983, p. 72)

The *administrator-centred* perspective relates to the efficiency of the school as an administrative organization. At Rivendell the dual structure of years and houses was criticized by several staff on the grounds of organizational complexity. One senior teacher thought that there was 'too much duplication. I just think it is sloppy, quite frankly . . . It should not be necessary to have more than twenty people in positions of authority, and in some schools it is starting to look like everyone is' (Best *et al.*, 1983, p. 76). A similar view was expressed by a junior member of staff:

> At the moment there are too many people; for example, a fifth-form tutor may have to contact Farley as Head of Humanities, Bailey as Head of Year, and Austen as Head of House, on a problem that a child has in Humanities. . . . This is an instance of increasing bureaucracy in schools.
>
> (Best *et al.*, 1983, p. 77)

Teachers who adopt an administrator-centred approach thus evaluate pastoral structures in terms of their administrative efficiency rather than their effectiveness as welfare systems.

The *subject-centred* perspective relates primarily to the academic role of the teacher. Staff are concerned with their work as subject specialists and have little regard to their pastoral responsibilities. The learning situation is perceived as one where distinct subjects are taught by specialists. Best *et al.* (1983, p. 78) describe the attitude adopted by one teacher at Rivendell:

> One teacher . . . stood out from the rest because of her tendency to emphasise her role as the teacher of a *subject* rather than as a teacher of pupils or a 'carer' for children. The pastoral arrangements of the school did not seem to hold any importance for her, and she was simply uninterested in her own pastoral role as a form tutor.

The five perspectives identified by the authors are conceptually distinct but few teachers fit neatly into a single category. Nevertheless, the classification provides a useful framework of analysis for pastoral care while serving as a valuable illustration of the subjective model. The study confirms the view of subjective theorists that the school is not a monolithic organization. Each teacher has an individual interpretation of the school and these meanings may cluster into broad perspectives as was the case at Rivendell.

## Subjective models: goals, structure, environment and leadership

### *Goals*

Subjective models differ from other approaches in that they stress the *goals* of individuals rather than the objectives of the institution or its subunits. Members of organizations are thought to have their own personal aims which they seek to achieve within the institution. The notion of organizational objectives, central to formal and collegial models, is rejected, as Coulson (1985, p. 44) suggests:

> It is not schools or organisations but people who pursue goals or aims. . . . Teachers, especially perhaps headteachers, hold and pursue their own personal goals within schools, and many of these may be only tenuously linked to the teaching-learning process. . . . These individual goals relate to the person's self-esteem, career advancement, and job satisfaction.

As Coulson suggests, individual goals may be related only tangentially to the organization. Often they are not concerned with wider institutional issues but reflect the personal wishes of the staff as individuals. Greenfield (1973, p. 568) argues that 'Many people do not hold goals . . . in the sense of *ends* that the organisation is to accomplish, but merely hold a set of beliefs about what it is *right* to do in an organisation.' The denial of the concept of organizational goals creates difficulties because teachers are usually aware of the purposes and aims of schools and colleges. Many staff acknowledge the existence of school-wide goals such as teaching all children to read or achieving a good record in public examinations. At a common sense level these are regarded as organizational objectives.

Greenfield (1973), p. 557) suggests that goals which appear to be those of the organization are really the objectives of powerful individuals within the institution: 'The goals of the organisation are the current preoccupations and intentions of the dominant organisational coalition.' In schools it is assumed that headteachers may possess sufficient power to promote their own purposes as the objectives of the institution. In this view, organizational goals are a chimera; they are simply the personal aims of the most powerful individuals. In this respect, subjective models are similar to political theories.

At Wroxham primary school in Potters Bar, Hertfordshire, it was widely acknowledged that school aims were really those of the headteacher, Frances Smith. Two teachers illustrate this view:

> 'The aims emanate from Frances and the outlook she brings to the school. I endorse the aims but I am still coming to terms with them'.

> 'I regard the aims as primarily the expectations of the head. Frances puts a lot of effort into being influential. She communicates specific expectations'.
>
> (Bush, 1988, p. 56)

This example supports the subjective view that organizational goals are really the personal aims of influential people within schools and colleges. The subjective model's emphasis on individual goals is a valuable counter to the formal assumption about 'organizational' goals.

## Organizational structure

Subjective models regard *organizational structure* as an outcome of the interaction of participants rather than a fixed entity which is independent of the people within the institution. Structure is a product of the behaviour of individuals and serves to explain the relationships between members of organizations. 'An organisation structure should be seen as something constructed and sustained through human interaction . . . Structure is a description of behaviour rather than a constraint upon it; structure describes what people do and how they relate' (Cuthbert, 1984, p. 60). Formal and collegial models tend to regard structure as a fixed and stable aspect of organizations while subjective theories emphasize the different meanings placed on structure by the individuals within the institution. The management team might be portrayed as a participative forum by the headteacher but be regarded by other staff as a vehicle for the one-way dissemination of information.

Teachers interpret relationships in schools and colleges in different ways and, in doing so, they influence the structures within their institutions. However, there are variations in the amount of power which individuals can wield in seeking to modify structure, as Ranson, Hinings and Greenwood (1980, p. 7) explain:

Organisational structures are shaped and constituted by members' provinces of meaning, by their deep-seated interpretive schemes, and by the surface articulation of values and interests. More accurately, however, structuring is typically the privilege of *some* organizational actors . . . The analytical focus then becomes the relations of power which enable some organisational members to constitute and re-create organisational structures according to their provinces of meaning.

In education, heads and principals are often able to impose their interpretations of structure on the institutions they lead. They can introduce a faculty structure to promote interdepartmental co-operation, for example, but the effectiveness of such a change depends crucially on the attitudes of the staff concerned. 'Organisations will change as rapidly (or as slowly) as the ideas of their members' (Crowther, 1990, p. 14).

Structural change alone may be ineffective if it lacks the support of the people within the organization, as Greenfield, (1973, p. 565) demonstrates:

Shifting the external trappings of organisation, which we may call organisation structure if we wish, turns out to be easier than altering the deeper meanings and purposes which people express through organisation . . . we are forced to see problems of organisational structure as inherent not in 'structure' itself but in the human meanings and purposes which support that structure. Thus it appears that we cannot solve organisational problems by either abolishing or improving structure alone; we must also look at their human foundations.

While accepting the strictures of Greenfield about the limitations of structural change, there are obvious difficulties in understanding and responding to numerous personal interpretations of situations in organizations. The elusive and variable nature of human meanings suggests that organizational change may be a slow and uncertain process because it depends primarily on an understanding of individual wishes and beliefs.

Subjective theorists may be more interested in processes and relationships than in structure. While structure relates to the institutional level, subjective models focus on individuals and their interpretations of events and situations. The emphasis is on small-scale issues of concern to people rather than the macro-level of organizational structure: 'The phenomenologist is less concerned with structures than with processes involved at the microcosmic level as groups construct new realities within the framework of relatively enduring institutions' (Hoyle, 1986, p. 14).

## *The external environment*

In subjective models little attention is paid to relationships between organizations and their *external environments*. This may be because organizations are not portrayed as viable entities. The focus is on the meanings placed on events by people within the organization rather than interaction between the institution and groups or individuals external to it. The notion of outside bodies exerting influence on the school or college makes little sense when subjective models claim that organizations have no existence independent of the individuals within them.

Where subjective models deal with the environment at all, the emphasis is on links between individuals within and outside the organization rather than external pressures on the total institution. The assumption that human behaviour stems from a personal interpretation of events raises the issue of the source of these meanings. Subjective theorists argue that they emanate from the external environment:

> The environment in which an organisation is located might usefully be regarded as a source of meanings through which members defined their actions and made sense of the actions of others.
>
> (Silverman, 1970, p. 126).

> The kinds of organisation we live in derive not from their structure but from attitudes and experiences we bring to organisations from the wider society in which we live.
>
> (Greenfield, 1973, p. 558)

In education, the interpretations of individuals may originate from several sources. For teachers a major influence is the socialization that results from their induction into the profession. A head of department at Pensnett Comprehensive school expresses this view: 'Personal aims are instilled through training and the early years of teaching together with the general nature and ethos of the school' (quoted in Bush, 1988, p. 58). The process of socialization may be reinforced through interaction with significant individuals outside the institution who emanate from the same professional background. These include OFSTED inspectors, local advisers and staff from higher education. These professional contacts may be less important in the era of self-managing schools but their historical influence has tended to produce shared meanings and values. A stronger view is advanced by Watkins (1983) who claims that professionalism is a covert method of control, ensuring that teachers accept the authority of heads and other senior professionals.

Teachers are also subject to personal influences such as their family, friends and members of clubs and societies external to the school. These sources may lead to a diversity of meanings. Greenfield (1973, p. 559) prefers to emphasize differences in interpretation rather than shared meanings.

> This notion of organisations as dependent upon meanings and purposes which individuals bring to organisations from the wider society does not require that all individuals share the same meanings and purposes. On the contrary, the views I am outlining here should make us seek to discover the varying meanings and objectives that individuals bring to the organisations of which they are a part.

Formal models stress the accountability of organizations, and senior staff within them, to certain groups and individuals in the external environment. Subjective theories give little attention to this issue but the focus is implicitly on the answerability of individual teachers rather than the accountability of the institution itself (Bush, 1994). Elliott *et al.*'s research (1979) suggests that accountability may be primarily to the individual's own beliefs and values. While the focus on individual accountability is legitimate because it is people who act, the subjective model fails to deal with the expectations of external groups and individuals who often require an explanation of institutional policies and practice.

## *Leadership*

The concept of *leadership* fits rather uneasily within the framework of subjective models. Individuals place different meanings on events and this applies to all members, whatever their formal position in the organization. People who occupy leadership roles have their own values, beliefs and goals. All participants, including leaders, pursue their own interests. A significant difference, however, is that leaders of organizations may be in a position to impose their interpretations of events on other members of the institution. Management may be seen as a form of control with heads and principals elevating their meanings to the status of school or college policy. These leaders may use their resources of power to require compliance with these interpretations even where other staff do not share those meanings.

Subjective theorists prefer to stress the personal qualities of individuals rather than their official positions in the organization. 'Situations require appropriate behaviours for their resolution and this can only be done by those best fitted to deal with them irrespective of their formal position or status in the organisation' (Gray, 1982, p. 41). This emphasis on the personal attributes of staff suggests that formal roles are an inadequate guide to behaviour. Rather individuals bring their own values and meanings to their work: 'I do not find it satisfactory to describe organisations solely in terms of position, roles and prescribed role behaviour. Different personalities will behave quite differently in similar circumstances and however strong structural pressures may be, the results may not be at all similar for two different personalities' (Gray, 1979, p. 126).

At The Pensnett school in Dudley, which was in a period of transition during the author's research in 1986 and 1987, several staff pointed to the contrast between official position and leadership behaviours:

'Leadership depends on personal qualities such as tact and making people feel at ease. A number of people have these qualities but because they are not needed in their current roles have limited opportunity to demonstrate them. This is due to the hierarchical structure of the teaching profession.'

'Some senior staff may be going through the motions and not exercising leadership.'

'There are people in "high places" who hold a position on paper but whose influence doesn't exist in practice.'

(Bush, 1988, p. 58)

These quotations illustrate the subjective view that leadership is a product of personal qualities and skills and not simply an automatic outcome of official authority. However, positional power remains significant as the Pensnett experience suggests. Perhaps the most effective leaders are those who have positional power *and* the personal qualities to command the respect of colleagues, a combination of the formal and subjective perspectives.

## The limitations of subjective models

Subjective models are prescriptive approaches in that they reflect beliefs about the nature of organizations rather than presenting a clear framework for analysis. Their protagonists make several cogent points about educational institutions but this alternative perspective does not represent a comprehensive approach to the management of schools and colleges. Subjective models can be regarded as 'anti-theories' in that they emerged as a reaction to the perceived limitations of the formal models. Greenfield is zealous in his advocacy of subjective approaches and his rejection of many of the central assumptions of conventional organizational theory.

Although subjective models introduce several important concepts into the theory of educational management, they have four significant weaknesses which serve to limit their validity:

1. Subjective models are *strongly normative* in that they reflect the attitudes and beliefs of their supporters. Greenfield, in particular, has faced a barrage of criticism, much of it fuelled by emotion rather than reason, for his advocacy of these theories. Willower, (1980, p. 7) for example, claims that subjective models are 'ideological' and attacks their supporters:

[Phenomenological] perspectives feature major ideological components and their partisans tend to be true believers when promulgating their positions rather than offering them for critical examination and test . . .

The message is being preached by recent converts who . . . now embrace it wholeheartedly and with the dedication of the convert.

This comment serves to illustrate the intensity of feeling engendered by Greenfield's challenge to conventional theory. Nevertheless, there is substance in Willower's criticism. Subjective models comprise a series of principles, which have attracted the committed support of a few adherents, rather than a coherent body of theory: 'Greenfield sets out to destroy the central principles of conventional theory but consistently rejects the idea of proposing a precisely formulated alternative' (Hughes and Bush, 1991, p. 241).

2. Subjective models seem to assume the existence of an *organization* within which individual behaviour and interpretation occur but there is no clear indication of the nature of the organization. It is acknowledged that teachers work within a school or college but these bodies are not recognized as viable organizations. Educational institutions are thought to have no structure beyond that created by their members. The notion of school and college objectives is dismissed because only people can have goals. So organizations are nothing more than a product of the meanings of their participants. In emphasizing the interpretations of individuals, subjective theorists neglect the institutions within which individuals behave, interact and derive meanings. 'The action approach tends to assume an existing system in which action occurs but cannot successfully explain the nature of the system' (Silverman, 1970, p. 142).

3. Subjective theorists imply that *meanings* are so individual that there may be as many interpretations as people. In practice, though, these meanings tend to cluster into patterns which do enable participants and observers to make valid generalizations about organizations. The notion of totally independent perceptions is suspect because individual meanings depend on participants' background and experience. Teachers, for example, emanate from a common professional background which often results in shared meanings and purposes. Ryan (1988, pp. 69–70) criticizes Greenfield's neglect of the 'collective': 'By focussing exclusively on the "individual" as a theoretical . . . entity, he precludes analyses of collective enterprises. Social phenomena . . . cannot be reduced solely to "the individual".

Subjective models also fail to explain the many similarities between schools. If individual perceptions provide the only valid definitions of organizations, why do educational institutions have so many common features? A teacher from one school would find some unique qualities in other schools but would also come across many familiar characteristics. This suggests that there is an entity called a 'school' which may evoke similar impressions amongst participants and observers. Hills (1980, p. 35) argues that much behaviour in organizations is unsurprising:

One of the most noteworthy features of the settings we term organisations (schools, hospitals, firms, universities and so forth) is that they are characterised by a high degree of order. One may have great difficulty in making refined predictions about the details of what goes on in such settings, but one rarely finds conditions so altered that he [*sic*] cannot recognise where he is.

4. A major criticism of subjective models is that they provide few guidelines for managerial action. Leaders are left with little more substantial than the need to acknowledge the individual meanings placed on events by members of organizations. Formal models stress the authority of heads to make decisions while pointing to the need to acknowledge the place of official groups such as management teams and governing bodies. Collegial models emphasize the desirability of reaching agreement with colleagues and providing opportunities for participation in decision-making. Political models accentuate the significance of building coalitions among interest groups in order to ensure support for policy proposals. Subjective models offer no such formula for the development of leadership strategies but the focus on the individual may provide some guidance. The leader may seek to influence individual behaviour through the application of motivation theory in order to produce a better 'fit' between the participant's personal wishes and the leader's preferences. This stance may help leaders but it is much less secure than the precepts of the formal model. As Greenfield himself acknowledges: 'This conception of organisations does not make them easy to control or to change' (Greenfield, 1980, p. 27).

## Conclusion: the importance of the individual

The subjective model has introduced some important considerations into the debate on the nature of schools and colleges. The emphasis on the primacy of individual meanings is a valuable aid to our understanding of educational institutions. A recognition of the different values and motivations of the people who work in organizations is an essential element if they are to be managed successfully. Certainly teachers are not simply automatons carrying out routine activities with mechanical precision. Rather, they deploy their individual skills and talents for the benefit of pupils and students: 'Few of us can see ourselves as smoothly functioning components of a vast machine' (Theodossin, 1983, p. 83).

Subjective models provide a significant new slant on organizations but the perspective is *partial*. The stress on individual interpretation of events is valid but ultimately it leads to a blind alley. If there are as many meanings as teachers, as Greenfield claims, our capacity to understand educational institutions is likely to be fully stretched. If individual meanings are themselves subject to variation according to the context, as Best *et al.* (1983) suggest, then the number of permutations is likely to be overwhelming.

In practice, however, interpretations do cluster into patterns if only because shared meanings emerge from the professional socialization undergone by teachers during training and induction. If there are common meanings, it is possible to derive some generalizations about behaviour. Best *et al.* (1983) adopted a subjective approach in their study of Rivendell but they were able to identify five distinct perspectives on pastoral care arising from the individual interpretations of 59 teaching staff.

The subjective perspective does offer some valuable insights which act as a corrective to the more rigid features of formal models. The focus on individual interpretations of events is a useful antidote to the uniformity of systems and structural theories. Similarly, the emphasis on individual aims rather than organizational objectives is an important contribution to our understanding of schools and colleges. Greenfield's work has broadened our understanding of educational institutions and exposed the weaknesses of the formal models. His admirers stress the significance of his contribution to organisational theory:

> Greenfield . . . has almost single-handedly led a generation of educational administration theorists to a new perspective on their work. It seems indisputable that a decade from now . . . Greenfield's work will be regarded as truly pioneering.
>
> (Crowther, 1990, p. 15)

> To understand Greenfield, whether one agrees with him or not, is to understand the nature of organizational reality better and to be better able to advance the state of the art.
>
> (Hodgkinson, 1993, p. xvi)

Despite these eulogies, it is evident that subjective models have supplemented, rather than supplanted, the formal theories Greenfield set out to attack. While his focus on individual meanings is widely applauded, the notion of schools and colleges as organizational entities has not been discarded. There is a wider appreciation of events and behaviour in education but many of the assumptions underpinning the formal model remain dominant in both theory and practice.

The search for a synthesis between formal models and Greenfield's analysis has scarcely begun. The battle of ideas has been aimed at victory rather than integration and there has been little love lost between the protagonists:

> The tension between the opposing positions . . . has never been resolved . . . no synthesis has been achieved . . . the game begun by Greenfield is still in play. Sides can be and are taken and still time cannot be called.
>
> (Hodgkinson, 1993, p. xiv)

> The epistemological assumptions underpinning the two perspectives are probably irreconcilable. The social theories which are expressed in each are incompatible at the extremes but possibly not in the more moderate versions of each.
>
> (Hoyle, 1986, p. 13)

One way of understanding the relationship between formal and subjective models may be in terms of scale. Formal models are particularly helpful in understanding the total institution and its relationships with external bodies. In education the interaction between schools and the LEA, for example, may be explained best by using bureaucratic and structural concepts. However, the subjective model may be especially valid in examining individual behaviour and relationships between individuals. 'The systems approach may be likened to a kind of aerial photograph which seeks to provide a broad overview; and the phenomenological approach to a variety of microscopic photographs in which detail is enlarged to aid perception' (Theodossin, 1983, p. 83). Formal and subjective models thus provide complementary approaches to our understanding of organizations. The official structure of schools and colleges should be examined alongside consideration of the individual behaviour and perceptions of staff and students. While institutions cannot be understood fully with out an assessment of the meanings of participants, these interpretations are of limited value unless the more formal and stable aspects of organizations are also examined.

# References

Best, R. E., Ribbins, P. M. and Jarvis, C. B. (1979) Pastoral care: reflections on a research strategy, *British Educational Research Journal*, Vol. 5, no. 1, pp. 35–43.

Best, R., Ribbins, P., Jarvis, C. and Oddy, D. (1983) *Education and Care*, Heinemann, London.

Bruce, D. (1977) The phenomenology debate, *Educational Administration*, Vol. 6, no. 1, pp. 114–17.

Bush, T. (1988) *Action and Theory in School Management*, E325 *Managing Schools*, The Open University, Milton Keynes.

Bush, T. (1994) Accountability in education, in T. Bush and J. West-Burnham (eds.) *The Principles of Educational Management*, Longman, Harlow.

Coulson, A. (1985) *The Managerial Behaviour of Primary School Heads*, Collected Original Resources in Education, Carfax Publishing Company, Abingdon.

Crowther, F. (1990) The pioneers in administration, *Practising Administrator*, Vol. 12, no. 3, pp. 14–15.

Cuthbert, R. (1984) *The Management Process*, E323 *Management in Post Compulsory Education, Block 3, Part 2*, Open University Press, Milton Keynes.

Elliott, J., Bridges, D., Ebbutt, D., Gibson, R. and Nias, J. (1979) School accountability: social control or dialogue, *Cambridge Accountability Project*, Interim Report to the Social Science Research Council.

Gray, H. (1979) Personal viewpoint: organisations as subjectivities, *Educational Administration*, Vol. 7, no. 2, pp. 122–9.

Gray H. L. (1982) A perspective on organisation theory, in H. L. Gray (ed.) *The Management of Educational Institutions*, Falmer Press, Lewes.

Greenfield, T. B. (1973) Organisations as social inventions: rethinking assumptions about change, *Journal of Applied Behavioural Science*, Vol. 9, no. 5, pp. 551–74.

Greenfield, T. B. (1975) Theory about organisations: a new perspective and its implications for schools, in M. Hughes (ed.) *Administering Education: International Challenge*, Athlone Press, London.

Greenfield, T. B. (1979) Organisation theory is ideology, *Curriculum Enquiry*, Vol. 9, no. 2, pp. 97–112.

Greenfield, T. B. (1980) The man who comes back through the door in the wall: discovering truth, discovering self, discovering organisations, *Educational Administration Quarterly*, Vol. 16, no. 3, pp. 26–59.

Greenfield, T. B. (1986) The decline and fall of science in educational administration, *Interchange*, Vol. 17, no. 2, pp. 57–80, Summer.

Hills, R. J. (1980) A critique of Greenfield's 'New Perspective', *Educational Administration Quarterly*, Vol. 16, no. 1, pp. 20–44.

Hodgkinson, C. (1993) Foreword, in T. B. Greenfield and P. Ribbins (eds.) *Greenfield on Educational Administration*, Routledge, London.

Holmes, M. (1986) Comment on 'The decline and fall of science in educational administration', *Interchange*, Vol. 17, no. 2, pp. 80–90, Summer.

Hoyle, E. (1981) *The Process of Management*, E323 *Management of the School, Block 3, Part 1*, Open University Press, Milton Keynes.

Hoyle, E. (1986), *The Politics of School Management*, Hodder and Stoughton, Sevenoaks.

Hughes, M. and Bush, T. (1991) Theory and research as catalysts for change, in W. Walker, R. Farquhar and M. Hughes (eds.) *Advancing Education: School Leadership in Action*, The Falmer Press, London.

Innes-Brown, M. (1993) T. B. Greenfield and the interpretive alternative, *International Journal of Educational Management*, Vol. 7, no. 2, pp. 30–40.

Ranson, S., Hinings, B. and Greenwood, R. (1980) The structuring of organisational structures, *Administrative Science Quarterly*, Vol. 25, no. 1, pp. 1–7.

Ribbins, P. M., Jarvis, C. B., Best, R. E. and Oddy, D. M. (1981) Meanings and contexts: the problem of interpretation in the study of a school, *Research in Educational Management and Administration*, British Educational Management and Administration Society, Birmingham.

Ryan, J. (1988) Science in educational administration: a comment on the Holmes-Greenfield dialogue, *Interchange*, Vol. 19, no. 2, pp. 68–70, Summer.

Silverman, D. (1970) *The Theory of Organisations*, Heinemann, London.

Theodossin, E. (1983) Theoretical perspectives on the management of planned educational change, *British Educational Research Journal*, Vol. 9, no. 1, pp. 81–90.

Watkins, P. (1983) *Class, Control and Contestation in Educational Organisations*, Deakin University, Victoria, Australia.

Willower, D. J. (1980) Contemporary issues in theory in educational administration, *Educational Administration Quarterly*, Vol. 16, no. 3, pp. 1–25.

# 7

# *Ambiguity Models*

## Central features of ambiguity models

Ambiguity models include all those approaches that stress uncertainty and unpredictability in organizations. The emphasis is on the instability and complexity of institutional life. These theories assume that organizational objectives are problematic and that institutions experience difficulty in ordering their priorities. Subunits are portrayed as relatively autonomous groups which are connected only loosely with one another and with the institution itself. Decision-making occurs within formal and informal settings where participation is fluid. Individuals are part-time members of policy-making groups who move in and out of the picture according to the nature of the topic and the interests of the potential participants. Ambiguity is a prevalent feature of complex organizations such as schools and colleges and is likely to be particularly acute during periods of rapid change. The definition indicated below incorporates the main elements of these approaches:

> Ambiguity models assume that turbulence and unpredictability are dominant features of organizations. There is no clarity over the objectives of institutions and their processes are not properly understood. Participation in policy making is fluid as members opt in or out of decision opportunities.

Ambiguity models are associated with a group of theorists, mostly from the United States, who developed their ideas in the 1970s. They were dissatisfied with the formal models which they regarded as inadequate for many organizations, particularly during phases of instability. March (1982, p. 36) points to the jumbled reality in certain kinds of organization:

> Theories of choice underestimate the confusion and complexity surrounding actual decision making. Many things are happening at once; technologies are changing and poorly understood; alliances, preferences, and perceptions are changing; problems, solutions, opportunities, ideas, people, and outcomes are mixed together in a way that makes their interpretation uncertain and their connections unclear.

Unlike some other perspectives, the data supporting ambiguity models have been drawn largely from educational settings. Schools and colleges are characterized as having uncertain goals, unclear technology and fluid participation in decision-making. They are also subject to changing demands from their environments. These factors lead March and Olsen (1976, p. 12) to assert that 'Ambiguity is a major feature of decision making in most public and educational organisations.'

Ambiguity models have the following major features:

1. There is a lack of clarity about the *goals* of the organization. Many institutions are thought to have inconsistent and opaque objectives. Formal models assume that organizations have clear purposes which guide the activities of their members. Ambiguity perspectives, by contrast, suggest that goals are so vague that they can be used to justify almost any behaviour. It may be argued that aims become clear only through the behaviour of members of the organization:

> It is difficult to impute a set of goals to the organisation that satisfies the standard consistency requirements of theories of choice. The organisation appears to operate on a variety of inconsistent and ill-defined preferences. It can be described better as a loose collection of changing ideas than as a coherent structure. It discovers preferences through action more often than it acts on the basis of preferences.
>
> (Cohen and March, 1974, p. 3)

Educational institutions are regarded as typical in having no clearly defined objectives. The discretion available to teachers enables them to identify their own educational purposes and to act in accordance with those aims for most of their professional activities. Because teachers work independently for much of their time, they may experience little difficulty in pursuing their own interests. As a result schools and colleges are thought to have no coherent pattern of aims:

> It may not be at all clear what the goals of the school are. Different members of the school may perceive different goals or attribute different priorities to the same goals, or even be unable to define goals which have any operational meaning. Thus while it is commonly expected that those who work in schools should have some overall purpose it is likely that the organizational context of many schools actually renders this either impossible or very difficult. Hence schools face an ambiguity of purpose, the result of which is that the achievement of goals which are educational in any sense cease to be central to the functioning of the school
>
> (Bell, 1989, p. 134)

2. Ambiguity models assume that organizations have a *problematic technology* in that their processes are not properly understood. Institutions are unclear about how outcomes emerge from their activities. This is particularly true of client-serving organizations where the technology is necessarily tailored to the needs of the individual client. In education it is not clear how pupils and students acquire knowledge and skills so the processes of teaching are clouded with doubt and uncertainty. Bell (1980, p. 188) claims that ambiguity infuses the central functions of schools:

Teachers are often unsure about what it is they want their pupils to learn, about what it is the pupils have learned about and how, if at all, learning has actually taken place. The learning process is inadequately understood and therefore pupils may not always be learning effectively whilst the basic technology available in schools is often not understood because its purposes are only vaguely recognised. . . . Since the related technology is so unclear the processes of teaching and learning are clouded in ambiguity.

3. Ambiguity theorists argue that organizations are characterized by *fragmentation* and *loose coupling*. Institutions are divided into groups which have internal coherence based on common values and goals. Links between the groups are more tenuous and unpredictable. Weick (1976, p. 3) uses the term 'loose coupling' to describe relationships between subunits:

> By loose coupling, the author intends to convey the image that coupled events are responsive, *but* that each event also preserves its own identity and some evidence of its physical or logical separateness. . . . their attachment may be circumscribed, infrequent, weak in its mutual effects, unimportant, and/or slow to respond . . . Loose coupling also carries connotations of impermanence, dissolvability, and tacitness all of which are potentially crucial properties of the 'glue' that holds organisations together.

Weick subsequently elaborated his model by identifying eight particularly significant examples of loose coupling that occur between:

- individuals;
- subunits;
- organizations;
- hierarchical levels;
- organizations and environments;
- ideas;
- activities;
- intentions and actions.

(Orton and Weick, 1990, p. 208)

The concept of loose coupling was developed for, and first applied to, educational institutions. It is particularly appropriate for organizations whose members have a substantial degree of discretion. Client-serving bodies such as schools and colleges fit this metaphor much better than, say, car assembly plants where operations are regimented and predictable. The degree of integration required in education is markedly less than in many other settings, allowing fragmentation to develop and persist.

4. Within ambiguity models *organizational structure* is regarded as problematic. There is uncertainty over the relative power of the different parts of the institution. Committees and other formal bodies have rights and responsibilities which overlap with each other and with the authority assigned to individual managers. The effective power of each element within the structure varies with the issue and according to the level of participation of committee members. The more complex the structure of the organization, the greater the potential for ambiguity. In this view, the formal structures

discussed in Chapter 3 may conceal more than they reveal about the pattern of relationships in organizations.

In education, the validity of the formal structure as a representation of the distribution of power depends on the size and complexity of the institution. Many primary schools have a simple authority structure centred on the head and there is little room for misunderstanding. In colleges and large secondary schools, there is often an elaborate pattern of interlocking committees and working parties. Noble and Pym's (1970, p. 436) classic study of decision-making in a college illustrates the ambiguity of structure in large organizations:

> The lower level officials or committees argue that they, of course, can only make recommendations. Departments must seek the approval of inter-departmental committees, these in turn can only submit reports and recommendations to the general management committee. It is there we are told that decisions must be made . . . In the general management committee, however, though votes are taken and decisions formally reached, there was a widespread feeling, not infrequently expressed even by some of its senior members, of powerlessness, a feeling that decisions were really taken elsewhere. . . . as a committee they could only assent to decisions which had been put up to them from one of the lower tier committees or a sub-committee . . . The common attribution of effective decision making to a higher or lower committee has led the authors to describe the decision-making structure in this organisation as an involuted hierarchy.

5. Ambiguity models tend to be particularly appropriate for *professional client-serving* organizations. In education, the pupils and students often demand inputs into the process of decision-making, especially where it has a direct influence on their educational experience. Teachers are expected to be responsive to the perceived needs of their pupils rather than operating under the direct supervision of hierarchical superordinates. The requirement that professionals make individual judgements, rather than acting in accordance with managerial prescriptions, leads to the view that the larger schools and colleges operate in a climate of ambiguity: 'I believe that large and complex, multipurpose, rapidly expanding or otherwise changing organisations are anarchic . . . So are organisations with a high degree of professionalisation among their rank and file; service-producing organisations probably fit this picture better than goods-producing enterprises do' (Enderud, 1980, p. 236).

6. Ambiguity theorists emphasize that there is *fluid participation* in the management of organizations. Members move in and out of decision-making situations, as Cohen and March (1986, p. 3) suggest: 'The participants in the organisation vary among themselves in the amount of time and effort they devote to the organisation; individual participants vary from one time to another. As a result standard theories of power and choice seem to be inadequate.' Bell (1989, pp. 139–40) elaborates this concept and applies it to education:

> The school consists of groups of pupils and teachers all of whom make a wide range of demands on the organization. By their very nature schools

gain and lose large numbers of pupils each year and . . . staff may move or change their roles . . . Membership of the school also becomes fluid in the sense that the extent to which individuals are willing and able to participate in its activities may change over time and according to the nature of the activity itself. In this way schools are peopled by participants who wander in and out. The notion of membership is thus ambiguous, and therefore it becomes extremely difficult to attribute responsibility to a particular member of the school for some areas of the school's activities.

Changes in the powers of governing bodies in schools in England and Wales following the 1986 and 1988 Education Acts add another dimension to the notion of fluid participation in decision-making. Lay governors now have an enhanced role in the governance of schools. Nominally, they have substantial responsibility for the management of staff, finance, external relations and the curriculum. In practice, however, they usually delegate their powers to the headteacher and school staff. The nature of delegation, the extent of the participation of individual governors in committees and working parties, and the relationship between the headteacher and the chair of governors, may be unpredictable elements of the relationship.

At Stratford grant-maintained school in East London, disagreement between the headteacher and chair of governors about the powers of the governing body led to the involvement of the Secretary of State and the courts. In this case, the chair wanted a level of participation in school management much greater than that expected in most other schools (Bush, Coleman and Glover, 1993). While this is an extreme case, it serves to illustrate the ambiguity of the relationship between full-time professionals and part-time lay governors in the management of the school.

. A further source of ambiguity is provided by the signals emanating from the organization's *environment*. There is evidence that educational institutions are becoming more dependent on external groups. Self-managing schools and colleges are vulnerable to changing patterns of parental and student demand. Through the provision for open enrolment, parents and potential parents are able to exercise more power over schools. Funding levels, in turn, are linked to recruitment through the pupil-related element of Local Management of Schools (LMS). Colleges also have their income related to levels of student recruitment and retention. The publication of examination and test results, and of OFSTED inspection reports, also serves to heighten dependence on elements in the external environment.

For all these reasons, institutions are becoming more open to external groups. In an era of rapid change, they may experience difficulties in interpreting the various messages being transmitted from the environment and in dealing with conflicting signals. The turbulence arising from the external context adds to the ambiguity of the decision-making process within the institution.

. Ambiguity theorists emphasize the prevalence of *unplanned decisions*. Formal models assume that problems arise, possible solutions are formulated and the most appropriate solution is chosen. The preferred option is then implemented and subject to evaluation in due course. Proponents of the ambiguity model claim that this logical sequence rarely occurs in practice. Rather the lack of agreed goals means that decisions have no clear focus. Problems, solutions and participants interact and choices somehow emerge from the confusion. Bell (1980, p. 190) discusses this concept in relation to schools:

> The taking of decisions and the solution of the problems cannot be based on some notion of common goals. . . . [they] are more likely to consist of linking together problems, solutions, participants and choices in conditions of ambiguity such that there are no criteria for making the connections. Hence the ideal solution and its related problem may not be linked.

Hoyle (1986, pp. 69–70) refers to Christensen's (1976) study of a Danish school in which three apparently firm decisions were made but none of these 'decisions' were implemented, apparently for four reasons:

- The outcome of a decision may be less important than the process.
- Implementation is in the hands of people who may not share the attitudes of the decision-making group.
- The high level of attention given to the making of a decision may not be sustained through to its implementation.
- Other problems absorb the energies of the organization as new crises arise.

In England and Wales, Becher (1989) refers to the 'implementation gap' in the introduction of the National Curriculum. Because it is statutory, Becher claims that its adoption was 'coercive':

> Coercion would seem a prompt and efficient means of putting any proposal into effect . . . [but] those who are required to carry out the resulting policies have no sense of ownership of them . . . They may elect to ignore them or at best to interpret them in ways that serve their own interests.
>
> (Becher, 1989, p. 54)

These examples serve to illustrate the problematic nature of the relationship between the decision-making process and the outcomes of that process. The rational assumption that implementation is a straightforward element in the decision process appears to be flawed. In practice, it is just as uncertain as the process of choice.

9. Ambiguity models stress the advantages of *decentralization*. Given the complexity and unpredictability of organizations, it is thought that many decisions should be devolved to subunits and individuals. Departments are relatively coherent and may be able to adapt rapidly to changing circumstances. Decentralized decision-making avoids the delays and uncertainties associated with the institutional level. Individual and departmental autonomy are seen as appropriate for professional staff who are required to exercise their judgement in dealing with clients. Successful departments are able to expand and thrive while weaker areas may contract or even close during difficult periods. Weick (1976, p. 7) argues that devolution enables organizations to survive while particular subunits are threatened:

> If there is a breakdown in one portion of a loosely coupled system then this breakdown is sealed off and does not affect other portions of the

organisation . . . when any element misfires or decays or deteriorates, the spread of this deterioration is checked in a loosely coupled system . . . A loosely coupled system can isolate its trouble spots and prevent the trouble from spreading.

While decentralization does have certain merits, it may be difficult to sustain when leaders are increasingly answerable for all aspects of the institution. Underperforming departments or units can be identified through the inspection process, and the publication of performance indicators, and this limits the scope for 'sealing off' the weak subunits. Rather, action must be taken to remedy the weakness if the institution is to thrive in a period of heightened market and public accountability.

## The garbage can model

The most celebrated of the ambiguity perspectives is the garbage can model developed by Cohen and March (1986). On the basis of empirical research, they conclude that ambiguity is one of the major characteristics of universities and colleges in the USA. They reject the sequential assumptions of the formal models in which decisions are thought to emanate from a rational process. Rather they regard decision-making as fundamentally ambiguous. They liken the process to that of a 'garbage can':

A key to understanding the processes within organisations is to view a choice opportunity as a garbage can into which various problems and solutions are dumped by participants. The mix of garbage in a single can depends partly on the labels attached to the alternative cans; but it also depends on what garbage is being produced at the moment, on the mix of cans available, and on the speed with which garbage is collected and removed from the scene.

(Cohen and March, 1986, p. 81)

In their analysis of decision-making, the authors focus on four relatively independent streams within organizations. Decisions are outcomes of the interaction of the four streams as follows:

1. *Problems*  problems are the concern of people inside and outside the organization. They arise over issues of lifestyle; family; frustrations of work; careers; group relations within the organization; distribution of status, jobs and money; ideology; or current crises of mankind as interpreted by the mass media or the next-door neighbour. All require attention. Problems are, however, distinct from choices; and they may not be resolved when choices are made.

2. *Solutions*  a solution is somebody's product. A computer is not just a solution to a problem in payroll management, discovered when needed. It is an answer actively looking for a question. The creation of need is not a curiosity of the market in consumer products; it is a general phenomenon of processes of choice. Despite the dictum that you cannot find the answer until you have formulated the question, you often do not know what the question is in organizational problem-solving until you know the answer.

3. *Participants* participants come and go. Since every entrance is an exit somewhere else, the distribution of entrances depends on the attributes of the choice being left as much as it does on the attributes of the new choice. Substantial variation in participation stems from other demands on the participants' time (rather than from features of the decision under study).

4. *Choice opportunities* these are occasions when an organization is expected to produce behaviour that can be called a decision. Opportunities arise regularly, and any organization has ways of declaring an occasion for choice. Contracts must be signed; people hired, promoted, or fired; money spent; and responsibilities allocated.

(Cohen and March, 1986, p. 82)

Cohen and March's analysis is persuasive. They argue that problems may well be independent of solutions, which may be 'waiting' for a problem to emerge. Participation in decision-making is fluid in many schools and colleges and the 'decision' emerging from choice opportunities may well depend more on who is present for that meeting than on the intrinsic merits of the potential solutions. French (1989, p. 32) illustrates the vagaries of fluid participation in decision-making:

Most of us have in our time attended staff meetings, working parties, committee meetings, faculty boards. They may have been important decision-making affairs. How many people attended? All the required staff? Not quite? Ms A sends her apologies, Mr B is ill, Mr C not seen all week . . . . Half way through this eminent event we were joined by Mr D and Ms E; then after one hour, two people left – . . . we eventually reached a decision.

Cohen and March regard the garbage can model as particularly appropriate for higher education but several of the concepts are also relevant for schools. The major characteristics of ambiguous goals, unclear technology and fluid participation often apply to secondary schools although they may be less evident in the primary sector.

The major contribution of the garbage can model is that it uncouples problems and choices. The notion of decision-making as a rational process for finding solutions to problems is supplanted by an uneasy mix of problems, solutions and participants from which decisions may eventually emerge. The garbage can model has a clear application to educational institutions where there are many participants with ready-made solutions to apply to different problems.

At the former Cambridgeshire College of Arts and Technology (CCAT) a group of staff were committed to the maintenance and development of part-time courses and pursued this 'solution' at various opportunities. In 1982 the former National Advisory Board for Local Authority Higher Education (NAB) invited colleges to indicate priorities within their existing higher education courses on the assumption of a 10 per cent reduction in funding. The potential cuts package was discussed at the College's Academic Planning and Resource Committee where advocates of part-time provision sought to exclude those courses from the package. They were largely successful in that full-time course took the brunt of the proposed cuts. The 'solution' of protecting and enhanc ing part-time courses was attached to the 'problem' of planning for a possible cut in resources: 'Staff who believe that part time vocational courses are at the heart of colleges like CCAT found in the NAB exercise a convenient vehicle for this view' (Bush and Goulding, 1984, p. 39).

## Applying the ambiguity model – Oakfields School

The ambiguity model is an important contribution to the theory of educational management. It is a descriptive and analytical model which sets out its proponents' views of how organizations are managed rather than a normative approach extolling the 'right' way to manage institutions. However, there are few empirical studies which employ a conceptual framework drawn from the ambiguity perspective. One important example is Bell's (1989) research at Oakfields, a newly amalgamated secondary school in the English East Midlands.

Oakfields was formed by the amalgamation of three schools as part of the LEA's strategy for dealing with falling pupil numbers. The new school opened with 1500 pupils but numbers were expected to fall to about 900 within five years with obvious implications for staffing levels. This uncertainty was aggravated by the teachers' union action which meant that planning could not be undertaken at the end of the normal school day. The new school also operated on two sites. These factors created a turbulent environment with a high degree of ambiguity.

Bell refers to a lack of clarity about school aims, technology and school membership. The new head identified the goals but these were not shared by all staff. Attempts to resolve differences of view were inhibited by the teacher action, as the headteacher indicates: 'You may not agree with some of the policies and procedures or even with the long term aims, but until we can discuss these I should like everyone to enforce them for all our sakes, but especially for the sake of the children' (Bell 1989, p. 135). Bell notes that the lack of clarity about aims emanated from different perceptions held by staff from each of the three constituent schools, particularly in respect of discipline and aspects of the curriculum. It was clear also that teachers' opinions about the nature of the former schools influenced their attitudes: 'Staff . . . interpretation of the goals of the new school, and their stance towards operationalizing those goals, owed as much to their perception of the three constituent schools as it did to any statement of intent from the head of Oakfields' (Bell 1989, p. 136). Disagreement about the technology of the school centred around teaching styles and about the relative merits of separate or integrated subjects in science and humanities.

The notion of school membership was highly problematic because many staff retained a loyalty to their former school rather than the newly amalgamated unit. This was particularly true of teachers at the former secondary school who returned to that school's site for certain lessons. The most potent example concerned the former head of the secondary school who was based at the satellite campus as 'associate head' and also influenced the views of several colleagues:

He could only be described as being a member of Oakfields school if the notion of membership is used to indicate the most tenuous of connections.

Several of his erstwhile colleagues took up a similar position to the extent that they were in the new school but not of it.

(Bell, 1989, p. 140).

The ambiguous aims, technology and membership were reflected in the decision-making process which was often unpredictable and irrational. Bell claims that Oakfields illustrates the limitations of formal theories and the salience of the ambiguity model:

> The traditional notion of the school as an hierarchical decision-making structure with a horizontal division into departments and a vertical division into authority levels needs to be abandoned. Such a conceptualization is unsuitable for the analysis of an organization attempting to cope with an unstable and unpredictable environment . . . The fundamental importance of unclear technology, fluid membership and the problematic nature and position of educational goals has to be accorded due recognition in any analysis of the organization and management of a school such as Oakfields.
>
> (Bell, 1989, p. 146)

## Ambiguity models: goals, structure, environment and leadership

### Goals

Ambiguity models differ from all other approaches in stressing the problematic nature of *goals*. The other theories may emphasize the institution or the subunit or the individual but they all assume that objectives are clear at the levels identified. The distinctive quality of the ambiguity perspective is that purposes are regarded not only as vague and unclear but also as an inadequate guide to behaviour: 'Events are not dominated by intention. The processes and the outcomes are likely to appear to have no close relation with the explicit intention of actors . . . intention is lost in context dependent flow of problems, solutions, people, and choice opportunities' (Cohen, March and Olsen, 1976, p. 37). Ambiguity theorists argue that decision-making represents an opportunity for discovering goals rather than promoting policies based on existing objectives. The specific choice situation acts as a catalyst in helping individuals to clarify their preferences: 'Human choice behaviour is at least as much a process for discovering goals as for acting on them' (Cohen and March, 1986, p. 220).

Hoyle (1986, pp. 69 and 71) argues that the broad aims of schools are usually very general and uncontroversial but that difficulties arise when these goals are translated into specific commitments. He claims that the concept of organizational goal is 'slippery' and appears to adopt an approach that combines the ambiguity and political models:

> [The ambiguity] approach takes over when it becomes a question of determining by what process particular goals become salient and what factors lead to choices being made . . . Although most schools will certainly move in some broad direction, the notion of a set of goals to which all the components are geared fails to correspond to the reality which is that insofar as a school has specific goals these will emerge from the interplay of interests within the school.

At The Pensnett school in Dudley the interplay of ambiguity and political approaches was clearly evident. The deputy head claims that the lack of clarity over goals was related to ideology:

> 'The aims are not universally understood. In particular there is misunderstanding over the community development aims of the school. This is in part a product of limited consultation within the school during the early stages of community development, and in part a consequence of conflicting ideologies of community development beyond the school.'
>
> (quoted in Bush, 1988, p. 62)

## Organizational structure

Ambiguity models regard *organizational structure* as problematic. Institutions are portrayed as aggregations of loosely coupled subunits with structures that may be both ambiguous and subject to change. In many educational organizations, and certainly in larger schools and colleges, policy is determined primarily by committees rather than individuals. The various committees and working parties collectively comprise the structure of the organization.

Enderud (1980, p. 248) argues that organizational structure may be subject to a variety of interpretations because of the ambiguity and subunit autonomy that exists in many large and complex organizations: 'What really matters to the way in which the formal structure influences the processes is not what the structure formally "looks like", but the way it is actually used.' Enderud (1980) points to four factors which influence the interpretation of structure:

1. Institutions usually classify responsibilities into decision areas which are then allocated to different bodies or individuals. An obvious example is the distinction made between the academic and pastoral structures in many secondary schools. However, these decision areas may not be delineated clearly or the topics treated within each area may overlap. A pupil's academic progress, for example, may be hampered by personal or domestic considerations. 'The result is that a given decision may quite reasonably be subject to different classifications of decision area. This again means that the circle of participants who are to deal with the matter is also open to interpretation' (Enderud, 1980, p. 249).
2. Decisions may also be classified in other ways. Issues may be major or minor, urgent or long-term, administrative or political, and so on. These distinctions offer the same opportunities for different interpretations as exist with delineation by area.
3. Rules and regulations concerning the decision process within the formal structure may be unclear. The choice of rules for decision-making is often subject to *ad hoc* interpretation. The adoption of a voting process, or an attempt to reach consensus or a proposal to defer a decision may be unpredictable and have a significant influence on the final outcome.
4. Rules and regulations may be disregarded in certain circumstances. Most organizational structures have elements designed to deal with emergencies or procedural conflicts. The formal structure may be circumvented to deal with particular occurrences where participants can agree on such practice.

A further source of ambiguity concerns the extent of *participation* within the organizational structure. Certain individuals within the institution have the right to participate in decision-making through their membership of committees and working parties. Cohen, March and Olsen (1976, p. 27) stress that committee membership is only the starting point for participation in decision-making: 'Such rights are necessary, but not sufficient, for actual involvement in a decision. They can be viewed as invitations to participation. Invitations that may or may not be accepted.' The elaborate participative structure at Churchfields High school in West Bromwich illustrates this point well. There are many committees which provide substantial opportunities for staff to influence decisions. In practice, however, teachers are selective about their participation in the decision process. One deputy head explains how staff use the structure: 'Individuals select certain items which interest them particularly and then they will make a statement and make their feelings known on that particular issue; but many day-to-day things go through on the say so of the headteacher' (quoted in Bush, 1993, p. 41). A basic assumption of ambiguity models is that participation in decision-making is fluid as members underuse their decision rights. One consequence of such structural ambiguities is that decisions may be possible only where there are enough participants. Attempts to make decisions without sufficient participation may founder at subsequent stages of the process.

## The external environment

The *external environment* is a source of ambiguity which adds to the unpredictability of organizations. Schools and colleges have a continuing existence only as long as they are able to satisfy the needs of their environments. So educational institutions have to be sensitive to the messages transmitted by external groups and individuals. Bell (1980, pp. 186–7) emphasizes that schools are dependent on elements within their environments:

> Perhaps it needs to be recognised more explicitly that organisations, including schools, sometimes operate in a complex and unstable environment over which they exert only modest control and which is capable of producing effects which penetrate the strongest and most selective of boundaries. . . . many schools are now unable to disregard pressures emanating from their wider environment. They are no longer able to respond to the uncertainty which such pressures often bring by attempting to buffer themselves against the unforeseen or by gaining control over the source of the uncertainty and thus restoring stability. The external pressures are, in many cases, too strong for that.

One example of externally-generated turbulence in schools was the teachers pay and conditions dispute in England and Wales in the mid-1980s which disrupted many school activities. The many unpredictable features of the dispute included the relatively short notice given in respect of strike action and the uncertainty about when the matter would be resolved. The headteacher of Wroxham primary school in Potters Bar expressed her concern in a report to the governing body:

> 'The school really felt the hardening of the teacher action last term. The junior children have missed the football and netball matches . . . as well as the other clubs. The lack of staff meetings is severely affecting communica

tion and has effectively brought to a standstill all curriculum discussion, an essential part of school development. Finally NUT strike action brought five classes to a halt on four occasions last term'

(quoted in Bush, 1988, p. 63)

The development of a 'market economy' in education means that schools and colleges have to be increasingly sensitive to the demands of clients and potential clients. Institutions which fail to meet the requirements of their environments may suffer the penalty of contraction or closure. The 1992 White Paper (DFE, 1992) in England and Wales makes it clear that the main criterion for closure will be parental demand for places. The demise of certain schools as a result of falling rolls may be regarded as a failure to satisfy market needs. Closure is often preceded by a period of decline as parents opt to send their children to other schools which are thought to be more suitable. One way of assessing these events is to view the unpopularity of schools as a product of their inability to interpret the wishes of the environment.

Another aspect of environmental turbulence concerns the reduced role of LEAs since incorporation of colleges, LMS and the provision for opting out. Schools and colleges are increasingly required to operate as self-managing units rather than as part of a wider educational service. The weakness of LEAs means that the local educational environment is much less predictable than it was in the 1980s.

These external uncertainties interact with the other unpredictable aspects of organizations to produce a confused pattern far removed from the clear, straightforward assumptions associated with the formal models. A turbulent environment combines with the internal ambiguities and may mean that management in education is often a hazardous and irrational activity.

## Leadership

In a climate of ambiguity traditional notions of *leadership* require modification. The unpredictable features of anarchic organizations create difficulties for the manager and suggest a different approach to the management of schools and colleges. According to Cohen and March (1974, pp. 195–203), leaders face four fundamental ambiguities:

1. There is an ambiguity of *purpose* because the goals of the organization are unclear. It is difficult to specify a set of clear, consistent goals which would receive the endorsement of members of the institution. Moreover, it may be impossible to infer a set of objectives from the activities of the organization. If there are no clear goals leaders have an inadequate basis for assessing the actions and achievements of the institution.
2. There is an ambiguity of *power* because it is difficult to make a clear assessment of the power of leaders. Heads and principals do possess authority arising from their position as the formal leaders of their institutions. However, in an unpredictable setting, formal authority is an uncertain guide to the power of leaders. Decisions emerge from a complex process of interaction. Leaders are participants in the process but their 'solutions' may not emerge as the preferred outcomes of the organization.

3. There is an ambiguity of *experience* because in conditions of uncertainty leaders may not be able to learn from the consequences of their actions. In a straightforward situation leaders choose from a range of alternatives and assess the outcome in terms of the goals of the institution. This assessment then provides a basis for action in similar situations. In conditions of ambiguity, however, outcomes depend on factors other than the behaviour of the leaders. External changes occur and distort the situation so that experience becomes an unreliable guide to future action.

4. There is an ambiguity of *success* because it is difficult to measure the achievements of leaders. Heads and principals are usually appointed to these posts after good careers as teachers and middle managers. They have become familiar with success. However, the ambiguities of purpose, power and experience make it difficult for leaders to distinguish between success and failure.

Cohen and March (1986, p. 195) point to the problems for leaders faced with these uncertainties:

> These ambiguities are fundamental . . . because they strike at the heart of the usual interpretations of leadership. When purpose is ambiguous, ordinary theories of decision making and intelligence become problematic. When power is ambiguous, ordinary theories of social order and control become problematic. When experience is ambiguous, ordinary theories of learning and adaptation become problematic. When success is ambiguous, ordinary theories of motivation and personal pleasure become problematic.

These ambiguous features imply that leaders cannot control the institution in the manner suggested by the formal models. Rather they become facilitators of a complex decision-making process, creating opportunities for the discussion of problems, the participation of members and the exposition of solutions.

Two alternative leadership strategies are postulated for conditions of ambiguity. One stratagem involves a participative role for leaders to maximize their influence on policy. Cohen and March (1986) and March (1982) suggest the following approaches for the management of uncertainty:

1. Leaders should be ready to devote *time* to the process of decision-making. By taking the trouble to participate fully, leaders are likely to be present when issues are finally resolved and will have the opportunity to influence the decision.

2. Leaders should be prepared to *persist* with those proposals which do not gain the initial support of groups within the institution. Issues are likely to surface at several forums and a negative reception at one setting may be reversed on another occasion when there may be different participants.

3. Leaders should facilitate the *participation of opponents* of the leader's proposals. Occasional participants tend to have aspirations which are out of touch with reality. Direct involvement in decision-making increases members' awareness of the ramifications of various courses of action. The inclusion of opponents at appropriate forums may lead to the modification or withdrawal of alternative ideas and allow the leader's plans to prosper.

4. Leaders should *overload the system* with ideas to ensure the success of some of the initiatives. When the organization has to cope with a surfeit of issues it is likely that some of the proposals will succeed even if others fall by the wayside.

These tactical manoeuvres may appear rather cynical and they have certain similarities with the political models discussed in Chapter 5. The alternative strategem is for leaders to forsake direct involvement in the policy-making process and to concentrate on structural and personnel matters.

Attention to the formal structure enables leaders to influence the framework of decision-making. In deciding where issues should be discussed there is an effect on the outcome of those discussions.

This second strategem also requires leaders to pay careful attention to the selection and deployment of staff. If heads or principals recruit teachers who share their educational philosophies then it is likely that their preferred solutions will become school or college policy. The structural and personnel aspects of management can overlap. Heads may encourage like-minded staff to join committees and working parties to improve the prospects of favourable outcomes. 'These policy recommendations amount to unobtrusive management in the extreme. The emphasis is on structural design and personnel selection, rather than tactical machinations' (Padgett, 1980, p. 602).

Both these strategies suggest that leaders in ambiguous situations should proceed by stealth rather than overt proclamation of particular policies. As Baldridge *et al.* (1978, p. 26) point out, the management of uncertainty requires different qualities from the management of bureaucracies:

> In such fluid circumstances . . . leaders serve primarily as catalysts. They do not so much lead the institutions as they channel its activities in subtle ways. They do not command, they negotiate. They do not plan comprehensively, they try to nudge problems together with pre-existing solutions. They are not heroic leaders, they are facilitators of an ongoing process.

While these strategies may be appropriate for periods of high ambiguity, the tensions inherent in turbulent organizations may be very stressful for heads and principals who have to absorb these pressures both to facilitate institutional development and to foster personal survival and growth. 'Successful heads have a high tolerance of ambiguity. Heads whose personal needs for structuring, continuity and stability are high may find frequent change and constant uncertainty a potent source of frustration and tension' (Coulson, 1986, p. 85).

## The limitations of ambiguity models

Ambiguity models add some important dimensions to the theory of educational management. The concepts of problematic goals, unclear technology and fluid participation are significant contributions to organizational analysis. Most schools and colleges possess these features to a greater or lesser extent, so ambiguity models should be regarded primarily as analytical or descriptive approaches rather than normative theories. They claim to mirror reality rather than suggesting that organizations *should* operate as anarchies.

The turbulence of educational policy in England and Wales during the late 1980s and 1990s lends credence to ambiguity theories. The rapid pace of curriculum change, and the unpredictable nature of school and college funding, lead to multiple uncertainty which can be explained adequately only within the ambiguity framework (Bush, 1994, p. 46). The ambiguity model appears to be increasingly plausible but it does have four significant weaknesses:

1. It is difficult to reconcile ambiguity perspectives with the customary structures and processes of schools and colleges. Participants may move in and out of decision-making situations but the policy framework remains intact and has a continuing influence on the outcome of discussions. Specific goals may be unclear but teachers usually understand and accept the broad aims of education. According to Padgett (1980), the ambiguity model 'seems curiously divorced from the familiar world of hierarchical authority, organisational differentiation, standard operating procedures, and centralisation policy known to us all'.

2. Ambiguity models exaggerate the degree of uncertainty in educational institutions. Schools and colleges have a number of predictable features which serve to clarify the responsibilities of their members. Students, pupils and staff are expected to behave in accordance with standard rules and procedures. The timetable regulates the location and movement of all participants. There are usually clear plans to guide the classroom activities of teachers and pupils. Staff are aware of the accountability patterns, with teachers responsible ultimately to heads and principals who, in turn, are answerable to governing bodies and the funding agencies.

   The predictability of schools and colleges is reinforced by the professional socialization which occurs during teacher training, induction and mentoring. Teachers assimilate the expected patterns of behaviour and reproduce them in their professional lives. Socialization thus serves to reduce uncertainty and unpredictability in education. Educational institutions are rather more stable and predictable than the ambiguity perspective suggests: 'The term organised anarchy may seem overly colourful, suggesting more confusion, disarray, and conflict than is really present' (Baldridge *et al.*, 1978, pp. 28).

3. Ambiguity models are not appropriate for stable organizations or for any institutions during periods of stability. Turner (1977) argues that the degree of predictability in schools depends on the nature of relationships with the external environment. Where institutions are able to maintain relatively impervious boundaries they can exert strong control over their own processes. Over-subscribed schools, for example, may be able to rely on their popularity to insulate their activities from external pressures.

4. Ambiguity models offer little practical guidance to leaders in educational institutions. While formal models emphasize the head's leading role in policy-making and collegial models stress the importance of team work, ambiguity models can offer nothing more tangible than unobtrusive management. 'Purposeful management is difficult to reconcile with problematic goals, unclear technology, and fluid participation' (Cuthbert, 1984, p.

58).Cohen and March (1986, p. 91) accept that their garbage can model has limitations while proclaiming its relevance to many organizations. 'We acknowledge immediately that no real system can be fully characterised in this way. Nonetheless, the simulated organisations exhibit behaviour that can be observed some of the time in almost all organisations and frequently in some.'

## Conclusion: ambiguity or rationality?

Ambiguity models make a valuable contribution to the theory of educational management. The emphasis on the unpredictability of organizations is a significant counter to the view that problems can be solved through a rational process. The notion of managers making a considered choice from a range of alternatives depends crucially on their ability to predict the consequences of a particular action. The edifice of the formal models is shaken by the recognition that conditions in schools and colleges may be too uncertain to allow an informed choice among alternatives.

In practice, however, educational institutions operate with a mix of rational and anarchic processes. The more unpredictable the internal and external environment, the more applicable is the ambiguity metaphor: 'Organisations . . . are probably more rational than they are adventitious and the quest for rational procedures is not misplaced. However, . . . rationalistic approaches will always be blown off course by the contingent, the unexpected and the irrational' (Hoyle, 1986, p. 72).

The emphasis on development planning provides a rational element in school and college management and a collective opportunity to tackle ambiguity and determine the institutional response to imposed change. The action plans required of school governing bodies following OFSTED inspections may also be regarded as a rational response to external turbulence. Wallace (1991, pp. 182 and 185) emphasizes that schools have to plan within a framework of uncertainty: 'The nature of many external innovations is liable to change unpredictably. It is in this rather frenetic context, which includes much ambiguity, that planning . . . must take place . . . the context for development planning [is] neither wholly chaotic nor entirely stable.'

The ambiguity model has much to offer but it has to be assessed alongside the formal perspective and other theories of educational management. On its own, it is not sufficiently comprehensive to explain behaviour and events in education. Its relevance is over-stated by its adherents but it does offer fascinating and valuable insights into the nature of school and college management:

In many ways the organized anarchy image is an exceptionally strong and persuasive concept. It breaks through much traditional formality that surrounds discussions of decision making. The imagery of organised anarchy helps capture the spirit of the confused organisational dynamics in academic institutions: unclear goals, unclear technologies, and environmental vulnerability. . . . the term helps to expand our conceptions, dislodge the bureaucracy image, and suggest a looser, more fluid kind of organisation.
(Baldridge *et al.*, 1978, p. 27)

# References

Baldridge, J. V., Curtis, D. V., Ecker, G. and Riley, G. L. (1978) *Policy Making and Effective Leadership*, Jossey Bass, San Francisco.

Becher, T. (1989) The national curriculum and the implementation gap, in M. Preedy (ed.) *Approaches to Curriculum Management*, Open University Press, Milton Keynes.

Bell, L. A. (1980) The school as an organisation: a re-appraisal, *British Journal of Sociology of Education*, Vol. 1, no. 2, pp. 183–92.

Bell, L. (1989) Ambiguity models and secondary schools: a case study, in T. Bush (ed.) *Managing Education: Theory and Practice*, Open University Press, Milton Keynes.

Bush, T. (1988) *Action and Theory in School Management*, E325 *Managing Schools*, The Open University, Milton Keynes.

Bush, T. (1993) *Exploring Collegiality: Theory and Practice*, E326 *Managing Schools: Challenge and Response*, The Open University, Milton Keynes.

Bush, T. (1994) Theory and practice in educational management, in T. Bush and J. West-Burnham (eds.) *The Principles of Educational Management*, Longman, Harlow.

Bush, T. and Goulding, S. (1984) *Cambridgeshire College of Arts and Technology: Facing the Cuts*, E324 *Management in Post Compulsory Education, Block 3, Part 4*, Open University Press, Milton Keynes.

Bush, T., Coleman, M. and Glover, D. (1993), *Managing Autonomous Schools: The Grant-Maintained Experience*, Paul Chapman Publishing, London.

Christensen, S. (1976) Decision-making and socialization, in J. G. March and J. P. Olsen, *Ambiguity and Choice in Organizations*, Universitetsforlaget, Bergen.

Cohen, M. D. and March, J. G. (1986) *Leadership and Ambiguity: The American College President*, The Harvard Business School Press, Boston MA. (First published 1974 by McGraw-Hill, New York.)

Cohen, M. D., March, J. G. and Olsen, J. P. (1976) People, problems, solutions and the ambiguity of relevance, in J. G. March and J. P. Olsen, *Ambiguity and Choice in Organisations*, Universitetsforlaget, Bergen.

Coulson, A. (1986) *The Managerial Work of Headteachers*, Sheffield City Polytechnic, Sheffield.

Cuthbert, R. (1984) *The Management Process*, E324 *Management in Post Compulsory Education, Block 3, Part 2*, Open University Press, Milton Keynes.

Department for Education (1992) *Choice and Diversity: A New Framework for Schools*, HMSO, London (The White Paper).

Enderud, H. (1980) Administrative leadership in organised anarchies, *International Journal of Institutional Management in Higher Education*, Vol. 4, no. 3 pp. 235–53.

French, B. (1989) *The Hidden Faces of Organisations: Some Alternative Theories of Management*, Sheffield City Polytechnic, Sheffield.

Hoyle, E. (1986) *The Politics of School Management*, Hodder and Stoughton Sevenoaks.

March, J. G. (1982) Theories of choice and making decisions, *Society*, Vol. 20, no 1, copyright © by Transaction Inc. Published by permission of Transaction Inc.

March, J. G. and Olsen, J. P. (1976) Organisational choice under ambiguity, in J G. March and J. P. Olsen *Ambiguity and Choice in Organisations*, Universitetsforlaget, Bergen.

Noble, T. and Pym, B. (1970) Collegial authority and the receding locus of power *British Journal of Sociology*, Vol. 21, pp. 431–45.

Orton, J. and Weick, K. (1990) Loosely coupled systems: a reconceptualization *Academy of Management Review*, Vol. 15, no. 2, pp. 203–23.

Padgett, J. F. (1980) Managing garbage can hierarchies, *Administrative Science Quarterly*, Vol. 25, no. 4, pp. 583–604.

Turner, C. (1977) Organising educational institutions as anarchies, *Educational Administration*, Vol. 5, no. 2, pp. 6–12.

Wallace, M. (1991) Flexible planning: a key to the management of multiple innovations, *Educational Management and Administration*, Vol. 19, no. 3, pp. 180–92.

Weick, K. E. (1976) Educational organisations as loosely coupled systems, *Administrative Science Quarterly*, Vol. 21, no. 1, pp. 1–19.

# 8

# *Cultural Models*

## Central features of cultural models

Cultural models emphasize the informal aspects of organizations rather then their official elements. They focus on the values, beliefs and norms of individuals in the organization and how these individual perceptions coalesce into shared organizational meanings. Cultural models are manifested by symbols and rituals rather than through the formal structure of the organization. The definition suggested below captures the main elements of these approaches:

> Cultural models assume that beliefs, values and ideology are at the heart of organizations. Individuals hold certain ideas and value-preferences which influence how they behave and how they view the behaviour of other members. These norms become shared traditions which are communicated within the group and are reinforced by symbols and ritual.

Cultural models have become increasingly significant in education since the first edition of this book was published in 1986 and this trend has prompted the inclusion of this new chapter. Harris (1992, p. 4) claims that educational writers attach considerable value to culture: 'Theorists argue that educational administration has a technical management aspect but is mainly about the culture within an organization. This culture includes the rituals which occur (or should occur) within an organization . . . Educational managers . . . are taken to be those capable of shaping ritual in educational institutions.' This extract demonstrates that culture may be both operational and normative ('occur or should occur') and that leaders have a central role in influencing culture.

The increasing interest in culture as one element in school and college management may be understood as another example of dissatisfaction with the limitations of the formal models. Their emphasis on the technical aspects of institutions appears to be inadequate for schools and colleges aspiring to excellence. The stress on the intangible world of values and attitudes is a useful counter to these bureaucratic assumptions and helps to produce a more balanced portrait of educational institutions:

Every organization has a formally instituted pattern of authority and an official body of rules and procedures which are intended to aid the achievement of those goals. However, alongside this formal aspect of the organization are networks of informal relationships and unofficial norms which arise from the interaction of individuals and groups working within the formal structure.

(Harling, 1989, p. 20)

The developing importance of cultural models arises partly from a wish to understand, and operate more effectively within, this informal domain of the values and beliefs of teachers and other members of the organization. Morgan (1986) and O'Neill (1994) both stress the increasing significance of cultural actors in management. The latter charts the appearance of cultural 'labels' and suggests why they have become more prevalent in the 1990s:

The increased use of such cultural descriptors in the literature of educational management is significant because it reflects a need for educational organizations to be able to articulate deeply held and shared values in more tangible ways and therefore respond more effectively to new, uncertain and potentially threatening demands on their capabilities. Organizations, therefore, articulate values in order to provide form and meaning for the activities of organizational members in the absence of visible and certain organizational structures and relationships. In this sense the analysis and influence of organizational culture become essential management tools in the pursuit of increased organizational growth and effectiveness.

(O'Neill, 1994, p. 116)

Beare, Caldwell and Millikan (1989, p. 173) claim that culture serves to define the unique qualities of individual organizations: 'An increasing number of . . . writers . . . have adopted the term "culture" to define that social and phenomenological uniqueness of a particular organisational community . . . We have finally acknowledged publicly that uniqueness is a virtue, that values are important and that they should be fostered.'

The international trend towards self-managing institutions reinforces the notion of schools and colleges as unique entities. It is likely that self-management will be accompanied by greater individuality and, in the United Kingdom, this is one of the explicit aims of the Government's educational policy. Caldwell and Spinks (1992) argue that there is 'a culture of self-management'. The essential components of this culture are the *empowerment* of leaders and their acceptance of *responsibility*.

Cultural models have the following major features:

1. They focus on the *values and beliefs* of members of organizations. These values underpin the behaviour and attitudes of individuals within schools and colleges but they may not always be explicit. In Nias, Southworth and Yeomans' (1989, p. 11) research in primary schools, beliefs were often difficult to discern: 'Because group members share and understand them, they have little need to articulate them. Many beliefs are indeed so deeply buried that individuals do not even know what they are.' The assumption of 'shared' values is reflected in much of the literature on culture: 'Shared meaning, shared understanding and shared sensemaking are all different ways of describing culture . . . These patterns of understanding also provide

a basis for making one's own behaviour sensible and meaningful' (Morgan, 1986, p. 128).

The sharing of values and beliefs is one way in which cultural models may be distinguished from the subjective perspective. While Greenfield (1973) and other subjective theorists stress the values of individuals, the cultural model focuses on the notion of a single or dominant culture in organizations. This does not necessarily mean that individual values are always in harmony with one another. Morgan suggests that 'There are often many different and competing value systems that create a mosaic of organizational realities rather than a uniform corporate culture' (Morgan, 1986, p. 127).

The existence of more than one culture is more likely in large, multipurpose organizations such as universities and colleges as Sergiovanni (1984, p. 8) suggests:

> Within the university there exist several subcultures each seeking to promote and maintain its values. To understand the university is to understand the nature of multicultural societies, and to administer the university requires that one deal with the web of conflict and tension which exists as several subcultures try to protect their way of life.

Multiple cultures may also exist in primary education. Nias, Southworth and Yeomans (1989) note that in relation to two of their case-study schools there were subgroups which had their own cultures separate from that held by their heads. Fullan and Hargreaves (1992, pp. 71–2) argue that some schools develop a 'balkanized' culture made up of separate and sometimes competing groups:

> Teachers in balkanized cultures attach their loyalties and identities to particular groups of their colleagues. They are usually colleagues with whom they work most closely, spend most time, socialize most often in the staffroom. The existence of such groups in a school often reflects and reinforces very different group outlooks on learning, teaching styles, discipline and curriculum.

2. Cultural models emphasize the development of *shared norms and meanings*. The assumption is that interaction between members of the organization, or its subgroups, eventually leads to behavioural norms that gradually become cultural features of the school or college: 'The nature of a culture is found in its social norms and customs, and that if one adheres to these rules of behaviour one will be successful in constructing an appropriate social reality' (Morgan, 1986, p. 129). Nias, Southworth and Yeomans' (1989, pp. 39–40) research shows how group norms were established in their case-study schools:

> As staff talked, worked and relaxed together, they began to negotiate shared meanings which enabled them to predict each others' behaviour. Consequently each staff developed its own taken-for-granted norms. Because shared meanings and ways of behaving became so taken for granted, existing staff were largely unaware of them. But they were visible to newcomers . . . Researchers moving between schools were constantly reminded of the uniqueness of each school's norms.

These group norms sometimes allow the development of a monoculture in a school with meanings shared throughout the staff – 'the way we do things around here'. We have already noted, however, that there may be several subcultures based on the professional and personal interests of different groups. These typically have internal coherence but experience difficulty in relationships with other groups whose behavioural norms are different. Wallace and Hall (1994, pp. 28 and 127) identify senior management teams (SMTs) as one example of group culture with clear internal norms but often weak connections to other groups and individuals:

> SMTs in our research developed a 'culture of teamwork' . . . A norm common to the SMTs was that decisions must be reached by achieving a working consensus, entailing the acknowledgement of any dissenting views . . . there was a clear distinction between interaction inside the team and contact with those outside . . . [who] were excluded from the inner world of the team.

In this respect cultural models are similar to collegiality where loyalty may be to a department or other subunit rather than to the school or college as an entity.

3. Culture is typically expressed through *rituals and ceremonies* which are used to support and celebrate beliefs and norms. Schools, in particular, are rich in such symbols as assemblies, prize-givings and, in many voluntary schools, corporate worship. Hoyle (1986, pp. 150 and 152) argues that ritual is at the heart of cultural models: 'Symbols are a key component of the culture of all schools . . . [they] have expressive tasks and symbols which are the only means whereby abstract values can be conveyed . . . Symbols are central to the process of constructing meaning.' Beare, Caldwell and Millikan (1989, p. 176) claim that culture is symbolized in three modes:

- *Conceptually or verbally*, for example through use of language and the expression of organizational aims.
- *Behaviourally*, through rituals, ceremonies, rules, support mechanisms, and patterns of social interaction.
- *Visually or materially*, through facilities, equipment, memorabilia, mottoes, crests and uniforms.

Wallace and Hall (1994, p. 29) refer to rituals developed by SMTs, including seating arrangements for meetings and social occasions for team members.

4. Cultural models assume the existence of *heroes and heroines* who embody the values and beliefs of the organization. These honoured members typify the behaviours associated with the culture of the institution. Campbell-Evans (1993, p. 106) stresses that heroes or heroines are those whose achievements match the culture: 'Choice and recognition of heroes . . . occurs within the cultural boundaries identified through the value filter . . . . The accomplishments of those individuals who come to be regarded as heroes are compatible with the cultural emphases.' Beare, Caldwell and Millikan (1989, p. 191) stress the importance of heroes (and anti-heroes) for educational organizations:

> The heroes (and anti-heroes) around whom a saga is built personify the values, philosophy and ideology which the community wishes to sustain

. . . The hero figure invites emulation and helps to sustain group unity. Every school has its heroes and potential heroes; they can be found among principals and staff, both present and past; among students and especially old scholars who have gone on to higher successes; and among parents and others associated with the school. Every school honour board contains hero material.

## Handy's Four Culture Model

Each school and college has its own distinctive culture, dependent on the mix of values, beliefs and norms prevalent in the organization. We have also noted that larger schools and colleges may have several cultures, associated with subunits, operating simultaneously. Each culture has its own features which differentiate one school from another and give it a unique ethos. However, it is possible to identify certain 'ideal types' of culture. Organizations may typify one of these models through most if not all of their characteristics. The best known typology is that by Handy (1985), applied to schools by Handy and Aitken (1986). He identifies four cultures as follows:

- Club culture.
- Role culture.
- Task culture.
- Person culture.

*The club culture*   this organization is illustrated by the spider's web. The person at the head of the organization is located at the centre of the web, surrounded by concentric circles of associates. The organization is there as an extension of the head. Club cultures are rich in personality and abound in mythical stories and folklore from the past. Their danger lies in the dominance of the central figure. It works well when the organization is relatively small and when the leader is good. Handy and Aitken (1986) suggest that some primary schools may be benevolent club cultures.

*The role culture*   this culture is best represented by the organization charts familiar to larger schools and colleges and discussed in Chapter 3. The formal structure is evident from the chart which identifies roles and assigns responsibilities largely on the basis of official position. Communications are formalized and go from role to role rather than person to person. Role organizations are suitable for periods of stability and for routine tasks but less appropriate when there is rapid change. The focus is on organizational design and people are trained to fulfil their specific role. Handy and Aitken (1986) claim that secondary schools are often role cultures and this also applies to some colleges.

*The task culture*   in task cultures, a group or team is applied to a problem or task. The task culture is usually warm and friendly because it is co-operative rather than hierarchical. It has certain similarities with the collegial model. This culture thrives in problem-solving situations but may be very time consuming. Working parties are examples of task cultures whereas standing committees are typical of role cultures. Handy's research (Handy and Aitken 1986 suggests that many primary teachers regard their schools as task cultures. Clark (1992, p. 65) illustrates the task culture in education: 'We seem to have abandoned committees and sub-committees in the last three years and gone in for many more working parties. These are set up, make reports and close down again quickly, then before you know it another one springs up on another problem.'

*The person culture* this culture puts the individual first and makes the organization the resource for individual talents. This is consistent with the subjective model. The managers of the organization are of lower status than the individual professionals whose talents are at the heart of the organization. Expert or personal power is decisive because the star individuals are critical to the success of the organization. Few schools or colleges can be typified as person cultures although it may apply to heads of very successful departments which perform exceptionally well. It is relevant within universities where the talents of individual professors may be vital in securing the organization's reputation and research income.

Handy and Aitken (1986) stress that cultures are not inherently good or bad because they are situational. The important point is that culture should be appropriate for the organization and the people within it.

Bennett (1993, p. 36) accepts that the Handy model is a useful representation of organizational forms but argues persuasively that it does not explain culture: 'I do not think it is actually about cultures . . . It seems to marry well with theories of management, and to provide a useful way of characterizing the structure of organizations. But it does not address what makes a particular school . . . what it is.' Despite Bennett's reservations, the Handy model is useful in connecting culture and structure. It shows how structure may represent certain aspects of culture but it does not explain how values and beliefs coalesce to create the distinctive cultures of individual schools and colleges.

## Cultural models: goals, structure, environment and leadership

### Goals

The culture of a school or college may be expressed through its *goals*. The statement of purposes, and their espousal in action, serve to reinforce the values and beliefs of the organization. Where goals and values are consistent the institution is likely to cohere: 'A clear description of the aims of a school, college or any section within it helps to provide a common vision and set of values. Well-stated aims will seize everybody's interest. Such aims will help in creating a strong culture' (Clark, 1992, p. 74). Clark suggests that the process of goal-setting should be linked to organizational values. The core values help to determine the vision for the school or college. The vision is expressed in a mission statement which in turn leads to specific goals. This essentially rational process is similar to that set out in the formal models but within a more overt framework of values.

Official goals are often vague and tend to be inadequate as a basis for guiding decisions and action. Much then depends on the interpretation of aims by participants. This is likely to be driven by the values of the interpreter. Where there is a monoculture within the organization, a consistent policy is likely to emerge. If there are competing cultures, or 'balkanization' (Fullan and Hargreaves, 1992), the official aims may be subverted by members of subunits who will interpret them in line with their own sectional values and goals.

## Organizational structure

*Structure* may be regarded as the physical manifestation of the culture of the organization. The values and beliefs of the institution are expressed in the pattern of roles and role relationships established by the school or college. Handy's four culture model (Handy and Aitken, 1986), discussed earlier, is the best known typology linking structure with the culture of the organization.

Morgan (1986, p. 131) argues that a focus on organizations as cultural phenomena should lead to a different conceptualization of structure based on shared meanings. He adopts a perspective similar to the subjective model in discussing the link between culture and structure:

> Culture . . . must be understood as an active, living phenomenon through which people create and recreate the worlds in which they live . . . we must root our understanding of organization in the processes that produce systems of shared meaning . . . organizations are in essence socially constructed realities that rest as much in the heads of their members as they do in concrete sets of rules.

Structure is usually expressed in two distinct features of the organization. Individual roles are established and there is a prescribed or recommended pattern of relationships between role holders. There is also a structure of committees, working parties and other bodies which have regular or *ad hoc* meetings. These official encounters present opportunities for the enunciation and reinforcement of organizational culture. Hoyle (1986, pp. 163–4) stresses the importance of 'interpretation' at meetings:

> Ostensibly formal meetings are called to transact school business either in a full staff meeting or in various subcommittees and working parties. But meetings are rich in symbolic significance both *as* meetings and in the forms they take . . . The teachers have the task of interpreting the purposes of the meeting and they may endow a meeting with functions which are significant to them.

The larger and more complex the organization the greater the prospect of divergent meanings leading to the development of subcultures and the possibility of conflict between them:

> The relationship between organizational structure and culture is of crucial importance. A large and complex organizational structure increases the possibility of several cultures developing simultaneously within the one organization. A minimal organizational structure, such as that found in most primary schools, enhances the possibility of a solid culture guiding all areas of organizational activity.
>
> (O'Neill, 1994, p. 108)

The development of divergent cultures in complex organizations is not inevitable but the establishment of a unitary culture with wide and active endorsement within the institution requires skilled leadership to ensure transmission and reinforcement of the desired values and beliefs (see 'Leadership' section below).

## The external environment

The external environment may be regarded as the source of many of the values and beliefs that coalesce to form the culture of the school or college. The professional background and experience of teachers yield the educational values that provide the potential for the development of a common culture. However, there is also the possibility of differences of interpretation, or multiple cultures, arising from the external interests, professional or personal, of teachers and other staff.

O'Neill (1994, p. 104) charts the links between the external environment and the development of organizational culture (see Figure 8.1). The environment is the source of the values, norms and behaviours that collectively represent culture:

> The well-being of schools and colleges depends increasingly on their ability to relate successfully to their external environments. As such they are open rather than closed systems. It is therefore fundamentally important that the organization is able to offer visible and tangible manifestations of cultural 'match' to that environment.

O'Neill (1994) argues that the existence of complementary values should be publicized to external groups in order to sustain their sponsorship and support. This stance is particularly significant for autonomous colleges and schools whose success, or very survival, is dependent on their reputation with potential clients and the community. Caldwell and Spinks (1992) stress the need for self-managing schools to develop a concept of marketing that allows for the two-way transmission of values between the school and its community.

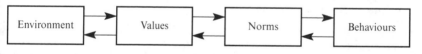

**Figure 8.1** The development of organizational culture

## Leadership

The leader of the organization has the main responsibility for developing and sustaining its culture. Heads and principals have their own values and beliefs arising from many years of successful professional practice. They are also expected to embody the culture of the school or college: 'Because of his [*sic*] formal authority the head represents and symbolises the school both to people inside it and to members of the community' (Coulson, 1986, p. 11). Hoyle (1986, pp. 155–6) stresses the symbolic dimension of leadership and the central role of heads in defining school culture:

Few heads will avoid constructing an image of the school. They will differ in the degree to which this is a deliberate and charismatic task. Some heads . . . will self-consciously seek to construct a great mission for the school. Others will convey their idea of the school less dramatically and construct a meaning from the basic materials of symbol-making: words, actions, artefacts and settings.

Nias, Southworth and Yeomans (1989, p. 103) suggest that heads are 'founders' of their school's culture. They refer to two of their case-study schools where new heads dismantled the existing culture in order to create a new one based on their own values. The culture was rebuilt through example: 'All the heads of the project schools were aware of the power of example. Each head expected to influence staff through his/her example. Yet their actions may also have been symbolic of the values they tried to represent.' Nias, Southworth and Yeomans (1989) also mention the significance of co-leaders, such as deputy heads and curriculum co-ordinators, in disseminating school culture.

Deal (1985, pp. 615–18) suggests several strategies for leaders who wish to generate culture:

- Document the school's history to be codified and passed on.
- Anoint and celebrate heroes and heroines.
- Review the school's rituals to convey cultural values and beliefs.
- Exploit and develop ceremony.
- Identify priests, priestesses and gossips and incorporate them into mainstream activity. This provides access to the informal communications network.

Leaders have the main responsibility for generating and sustaining culture and communicating its core values and beliefs both within the organization and to external stakeholders. Maintenance of the culture is regarded as a central feature of effective leadership. Sergiovanni (1984, p. 9) claims that the cultural aspect is the most important dimension of leadership. Within his 'leadership forces hierarchy', the cultural element is more significant than the technical, human and educational aspects of leadership:

> The net effect of the cultural force of leadership is to bond together students, teachers, and others as believers in the work of the school . . . . As persons become members of this strong and binding culture, they are provided with opportunities for enjoying a special sense of personal importance and significance.

## Limitations of Cultural Models

Cultural models add several useful elements to the analysis of school and college management. The focus on the informal dimension is a valuable counter to the rigid and official components of the formal models. By stressing the values and beliefs of participants, cultural models reinforce the human aspects of management rather than their structural elements. The emphasis on the symbols of the organization is also a valuable contribution to management theory. However, the cultural model does have three significant weaknesses:

1. There may be ethical dilemmas in espousing the cultural model because it may be regarded as the imposition of a culture by leaders on other members of the organization. The search for a monoculture may mean subordinating the values and beliefs of some participants to those of leaders or the dominant group. 'Shared' cultures may be simply the values of leaders imposed on less powerful participants. Morgan (1986, pp. 138–9) refers to 'a process of ideological control' and warns of the risk of 'manipulation': 'Ideological manipulation and control is being advocated as an essential managerial strategy . . . such manipulation may well be accompanied by resistance, resentment and mistrust . . . where the culture controls rather than expresses human character, the metaphor may thus prove quite manipulative and totalitarian in its influence.'

2. The cultural model may be unduly mechanistic, assuming that leaders can determine the culture of the organization (Morgan, 1986). While they have influence over the evolution of culture by espousing desired values, they cannot ensure the emergence of a monoculture. As we have seen, secondary schools and colleges may have several subcultures operating in departments and other sections. This is not necessarily dysfunctional because successful subunits are vital components of thriving institutions.

   In an era of self-managing schools and colleges, lay influences on policy are increasingly significant. Governing bodies have the formal responsibility for major decisions and they share in the creation of institutional culture. This does not mean simple acquiescence to the values of the head or principal. Rather, there may be negotiation leading to the possibility of conflict and the adoption of policies inconsistent with the leader's own values. Nias, Southworth and Yeomans (1989) refer to the dissatisfaction of two heads who experienced difficulty in gaining acceptance for their preferred ways of working.

3. The cultural model's focus on symbols such as rituals and ceremonies may mean that other elements of organizations are underestimated. The symbols may misrepresent the reality of the school or college. Hoyle (1986, p. 166) illustrates this point by reference to 'innovation without change'. He suggests that schools may go through the appearance of change but the reality continues as before:

   > A symbol can represent something which is 'real' in the sense that it . . . acts as a surrogate for reality . . . there will be a mutual recognition by the parties concerned that the substance has not been evoked but they are nevertheless content to sustain the fiction that it has if there has been some symbolisation of the substance . . . in reality the system carries on as formerly.

## Conclusion: values and action

The cultural model is a valuable addition to our understanding of organizations. The recognition that school and college development needs to be preceded by attitudinal change is salutary and consistent with the oft-stated maxim that teachers must feel 'ownership' of change if it is to be implemented effectively. Externally imposed innovation often fails because it is out of tune with the values of the teachers who have to implement it. 'Since organization ultimately resides in the heads of the people involved, effective organizational change implies cultural change' (Morgan, 1986, p. 138).

The emphasis on values and symbols may also help to balance the focus on structure and process in many of the other models. The informal world of norms and ritual behaviour may be just as significant as the formal elements of schools and colleges. Morgan (1986, p. 135) stresses the symbolic aspects of apparently rational phenomena such as meetings: 'Numerous organizational structures and practices embody patterns of subjective meaning that are crucial for understanding how organization functions day by day. For example meetings are more than just meetings. They carry important aspects of organizational culture.' As Morgan implies, cultural models have much in common with the subjective theories discussed in Chapter 6. The main difference is that cultural perspectives assume the emergence of shared meanings within the organization or subunit while Greenfield (1973) emphasizes individual interpretation of organizational phenomena.

Cultural models also provide a focus for organizational action, a dimension that is largely absent from the subjective perspective. Leaders may focus on influencing values so that they become closer to, if not identical with, their own beliefs. In this way, they hope to achieve widespread support for, or 'ownership' of, new policies. By working through this informal domain, rather than imposing change through positional authority or political processes, heads and principals are more likely to gain support for innovation. An appreciation of the salience of values and beliefs, and the ritual that underpins them, is an important element in the management of schools and colleges.

# References

Beare, H., Caldwell, B. and Millikan, R (1989) *Creating an Excellent School: Some New Management Techniques*, Routledge, London.

Bennett, N. (1993) *Effectiveness and the Culture of the School, E326 Managing Schools: Challenge and Response*, The Open University, Milton Keynes.

Caldwell, B. and Spinks, J. (1992) *Leading the Self-Managing School*, The Falmer Press, London.

Campbell-Evans, G. (1993) A values perspective on school-based management, in C. Dimmock (ed.) *School-Based Management and School Effectiveness*, Routledge, London.

Clark, J. (1992) *Management in Education*, Framework Press, Lancaster.

Coulson, A. (1986) *The Managerial Work of Primary School Headteachers*, Sheffield City Polytechnic, Sheffield.

Deal, T. (1985) The symbolism of effective schools, *Elementary School Journal*, Vol. 85, no. 5, pp. 605–20.

Fullan, M. and Hargreaves, A. (1992) *What's Worth Fighting for in Your School?*, Open University Press, Buckingham.

Greenfield, T. B. (1973) Organisations as social inventions: rethinking assumptions about change, *Journal of Applied Behavioural Science*, Vol. 9, no. 5, pp. 551–74.

Handy, C. (1985) *Understanding Organization*, Penguin, London.

Handy, C. and Aitken, R. (1986) *Understanding Schools as Organizations*, Penguin, London.

Harling, P. (1989) The organizational framework for educational leadership, in T. Bush (ed.) *Managing Education: Theory and Practice*, Open University Press, Milton Keynes.

Harris, C. (1992) Ritual and educational management: a methodology, *International Journal of Educational Management*, Vol. 6, no. 1, pp. 4–9.

Hoyle, E. (1986) *The Politics of School Management*, Hodder and Stoughton, Sevenoaks.

Morgan, G. (1986) *Images of Organization*, Sage, Newbury Park, California.

Nias, J., Southworth, G. and Yeomans, R. (1989) *Staff Relationships in the Primary School*, Cassell, London.

O'Neill, J. (1994) Organizational structure and culture, in T. Bush and J. West-Burnham (eds.) *The Principles of Educational Management*, Longman, Harlow.

Sergiovanni, T. (1984) Cultural and competing perspectives in administrative theory and practice, in T. Sergiovanni and J. Corbally (eds.) *Leadership and Organizational Culture*, University of Illinois Press, Chicago.

Wallace, M. and Hall, V. (1994) *Inside the SMT: Teamwork in Secondary School Management*, Paul Chapman Publishing, London.

# 9

# Conclusion: Towards a Comprehensive Model

## The models compared

The six models discussed in this book represent different ways of looking at educational institutions. They are analogous to windows, offering a view of life in schools or colleges. Each screen offers valuable insights into the nature of management in education but none provides a complete picture. The six approaches are all valid analyses but their relevance varies according to the context. Each event, situation or problem may be best understood by using one or more of these models but no organization can be explained by using only one approach. In certain circumstances a particular model may appear to be applicable while another theory may seem more appropriate in a different setting. There is no single perspective capable of presenting a total framework for our understanding of educational institutions, as Baldridge *et al.* (1978, p. 28) demonstrate:

> the search for an all-encompassing model is simplistic, for no one model can delineate the intricacies of decision processes in complex organisations such as universities and colleges . . . there is a pleasant parsimony about having a single model that summarises a complicated world for us. This is not bad except when we allow our models to blind us to important features of the organisation.

The formal models dominated the early stages of theory development in educational management. Formal structure, rational decision-making and 'top-down' leadership were regarded as the central concepts of effective management and attention was given to refining these processes to increase efficiency. Since the 1970s, however, there has been a gradual realization that formal models are 'at best partial and at worst grossly deficient' (Chapman, 1993, p. 215).

The other five models featured in this volume all developed in response to the perceived weaknesses of what was then regarded as 'conventional theory'. They have demonstrated the limitations of the formal models and put in place alternative conceptualizations that provide different portrayals of school and college management. While these more recent models are all valid, they are just as partial as the formerly dominant perspective their advocates seek to replace. There is more theory and, by exploring different dimensions of management, its total explanatory power is greater than that provided by any single model: 'Traditional views . . . still dominate understandings of theory, research and administrative practice [but] there are now systematic alternatives to this approach. As a result, educational administration is now theoretically much richer, more diverse and complex than at any other time in its short history' (Evers and Lakomski, 1991, p. 99).

The six models presented in this book are broad categories, encompassing a bewildering variety of different perspectives on management in education. Each has elements that provide a 'shock of recognition' and seem to be essential components of theory.

Collegial models are attractive because they advocate teacher participation in decision-making. The author's experience in postgraduate teaching, and as a consultant, suggests that most heads aspire to collegiality, a claim which rarely survives rigorous scrutiny. The collegial framework all too often provides the setting for political activity or 'top-down' decision-making.

The cultural model's stress on values and beliefs, and the subjective theorists' emphasis on the significance of individual meanings, also appear to be both plausible and ethical. In practice, however, these may lead to manipulation as leaders seek to impose their own values on their school or college.

The increasing complexity of the educational context may appear to lend support to the ambiguity model with its emphasis on turbulence and anarchy. However, this approach provides few guidelines for managerial action and leads to the view that 'there has to be a better way'.

The six models differ along crucial dimensions but taken together they do provide a comprehensive picture of the nature of management in educational institutions. We have chosen to emphasize four main aspects of management in organizations. A review of these elements provides a useful focus for a comparative analysis of the six perspectives.

## Goals

There are significant differences in the assumptions made about the *goals* of educational organizations. Formal models aver that objectives are set at the institutional level. It is thought that goals are determined by senior staff and the support of other teachers is taken for granted. The activities of schools and colleges are evaluated in the light of these official purposes.

The advocates of collegial models claim that members of an organization agree on its goals. These approaches have a harmony bias in that they assume that it is always possible for staff to reach agreement based on common values. Unlike formal perspectives the aims are not imposed from above but emerge from a participative process.

Political models differ from both the formal and collegial perspectives in stressing the goals of subunits or departments rather than those of the institution. There is assumed to be conflict as groups seek to promote their purposes. Goals are unstable as subunits engage in negotiation and alliances form and break down.

Subjective models emphasize the goals of individuals rather than institutional or group purposes. The concept of organizational objectives is supplanted by the view that individuals have personal aims. Schools and colleges are regarded as the subjective creations of the people within them and the only reality is their individual perceptions of the organization. Goals attributed to organizations are thought to be the purposes of the most powerful individuals within them.

Ambiguity theorists claim that goals are problematic. While other perspectives assume that objectives are clear at institutional, group or individual levels, the ambiguity approach assumes that goals are opaque. Aims are also regarded as an unreliable guide to behaviour. In this view it is mistaken to regard policies or events as a corollary of the goals of the institution.

In cultural models, goals are an expression of the culture of the organization. The statement of purposes, and their espousal in action, serve to reinforce the beliefs of the organization. The core values help to determine the vision for the school or college. This vision is expressed in a mission statement which in turn leads to specific goals.

## Organizational structure

The notion of *organizational structure* takes on different meanings within the various perspectives. Formal and collegial models regard structures as objective realities. Individuals hold defined positions in the organization and working relationships are assumed to be strongly influenced by these official positions. Formal models treat structures as hierarchical with decision-making as a 'top-down' process. Collegial models present structures as lateral with all members having the right to participate in the decision process.

Political models portray structure as one of the unstable and conflictual elements of the institution. The design of the structure is thought to reflect the interests of the dominant groups and individuals within the school or college. Committees and working parties may provide the framework for conflict between interest groups anxious to promote their policy objectives.

Subjective models regard organizational structure as a fluid concept that arises from relationships between individuals rather than an established framework constraining the behaviour of its members. The emphasis is on the participants rather than the roles they occupy. The interaction of people within the organization is reflected in the structure which is valid only as long as it accurately represents those relationships.

Ambiguity models assume that organizational structure is problematic because of the uncertain nature of the relationships between loosely coupled subunits. It may not be clear which group has the power to determine outcomes. Committees and working parties are characterized by the fluid participation of their members. Attendance is variable and decisions may be compromised by the absence of certain individuals who may challenge outcomes on other occasions.

In cultural models, structure may be regarded as the physical manifestation of the culture of the organization. The values and beliefs of the institution are thought to be expressed in the pattern of roles and role relationships established by the school or college. Committee meetings provide opportunities for the enunciation and reinforcement of organizational culture.

## The external environment

Relations with external groups are an increasingly important consideration for educational institutions if they are to survive and prosper. These links with the *environment* are portrayed in very different ways by the various models. Some of the formal approaches tend to regard schools and colleges as 'closed systems', relatively impervious to outside influences. Other formal theories typify educational organizations as 'open systems', responding to the needs of their communities and building a positive image to attract new clients.

Collegial models tend to be inadequate in explaining relationships with the environment. Policy is thought to be determined within a participatory framework which can make it difficult to locate responsibility for decisions. Heads may be held accountable for outcomes which do not enjoy their personal support, a position which is difficult to sustain for both the leader and the external group. Collegial approaches gloss over this difficulty by the unrealistic assumption that heads are always in agreement with decisions.

Political models tend to portray relationships with the environment as unstable. External bodies are regarded as interest groups which may participate in the complex bargaining process that characterizes decision-making. Internal and external groups may form alliances to press for the adoption of certain policies. Interaction with the environment is seen as a central aspect of an essentially political decision process.

In subjective models, the environment is treated as a prime source of the meanings placed on events by people within the organization. Individuals are thought to interpret situations in different ways and these variations in meaning are attributed in part to the different external influences upon participants.

Ambiguity models regard the environment as a source of the uncertainty which contributes to the unpredictability of organizations. The signals from outside groups are often unclear and contradictory, leading to confusion inside schools and colleges. Interpretation of messages from a turbulent environment may be difficult, adding to the ambiguity of the decision process.

In cultural models, the external environment may be regarded as the source of many of the values and beliefs that coalesce to form the culture of the school or college. The professional background and experience of teachers yield the educational values that provide the potential for the development of a common culture. However, there is also the possibility of multiple cultures arising from the divergent external interests, professional or personal, of teachers and other staff.

## Leadership

The perceived styles of *leadership* inevitably reflect the particular features of the diverse models of management. Within formal perspectives, the official leader is thought to have the major role in goal-setting, decision-making and policy formulation. Heads and principals are located at the apex of a hierarchy and they are acknowledged as the leaders both inside and outside the institution. The leader is assumed to be the most powerful person in the organization.

In collegial models, policies are thought to emerge from a complex process of discussion at committees and in other formal and informal settings. Influence is distributed widely within the institution and the leader is one participant in a collegial style of decision-making. Heads are assumed to have the prime responsibility for the promotion of consensus among their fellow professionals. A hierarchical approach is thought to be inappropriate for participative organizations and the leader is portrayed as *primus inter pares*.

Political models assume that leaders are active participants in the process of bargaining and negotiation which characterizes decision-making in organizations. Heads and principals have significant resources of power which they are able to deploy in support of their interests and objectives. Leaders may also mediate between groups in order to develop acceptable policy outcomes.

Subjective models de-emphasize the concept of leadership, preferring to stress the personal attributes of individuals rather than their official positions in the organization. All participants, including leaders, are assumed to have their own values and objectives which necessarily influence their interpretation of events. Heads and principals may be able to exert control over colleagues by enunciating institutional policies in line with their own personal interests and requiring the compliance of staff with these interpretations.

Ambiguity models stress the uncertainty facing leaders and the difficulties associated with the management of unpredictability. There are two schools of thought about the most appropriate leadership strategies for conditions of ambiguity. One mode involves active participation, with the leader engaging in various tactical machinations, an approach similar to that assumed in the political models. The alternative stance is to adopt an unobtrusive style with an emphasis on personnel and structural issues. Here the leader sets the framework for decision-making but avoids direct involvement in the policy-making process.

In cultural models, the leader of the organization has the main responsibility for developing and sustaining its culture. Heads and principals have their own values and beliefs arising from many years of successful professional practice and these may become the fulcrum of institutional culture. Leaders are expected to communicate the organization's core values and beliefs, both internally and to external stakeholders. Promotion and maintenance of the culture are regarded as central features of effective leadership.

The six perspectives differ significantly in the ways in which they treat the various components of institutional management, including goals, structure, environment and leadership. The major features of the six models are identified and compared in Figure 9.1.[1]

## Applying the models to schools and colleges

The six models represent conceptually distinct approaches to the management of educational institutions. However, it is rare for a single theory to capture the

1 Figure 9.1 has certain similarities with Cuthbert's (1984) tabular representation of five models using the criteria noted on page 24 above.

Type of model

| Elements of management | Formal | Collegial | Political | Subjective | Ambiguity | Cultural |
|---|---|---|---|---|---|---|
| Level at which goals are determined | Institutional | Institutional | Subunit | Individual | Unclear | Institutional or subunit |
| Process by which goals are determined | Set by leaders | Agreement | Conflict | Problematic May be imposed by leaders | Unpredictable | Based on collective values |
| Relationship between goals and decisions | Decisions based on goals | Decisions based on agreed goals | Decisions based on goals of dominant coalitions | Individual behaviour based on personal objectives | Decisions unrelated to goals | Decisions based on goals of the organisation or its subunits |
| Nature of decision process | Rational | Collegial | Political | Personal | Garbage can | Rational within a framework of values |
| Nature of structure | Objective reality hierarchial | Objective reality Lateral | Setting for subunit conflict | Constructed through human interaction | Problematic | Physical manifestation of culture |
| Links with environment | May be 'closed' or 'open' Head accountable | Accountability blurred by shared decision making | Unstable external bodies portrayed as interest groups | Source of individual meanings | Source of uncertainty | Source of values and beliefs |
| Style of leadership | Head establishes goals and initiates policy | Head seeks to promote consensus | Head is both participant and mediator | Problematic May be perceived as a form of control | May be tactical or unobtrusive | Symbolic |

**Figure 9.1**

reality of management in any particular school or college. Rather, aspects of several perspectives are present in different proportions within each institution. The applicability of each approach may vary with the event, the situation and the participants. The validity of the various models also depends on five overlapping considerations:

1. Size of the institution.
2. Organizational structure.
3. Time available for management.
4. The availability of resources.
5. The external environment.

We first examine the impact of institutional size.

1. *Size of the institution*   the size of the organization is an important influence on the nature of management structure and process. A small two teacher primary school necessarily operates very differently from a large multipurpose college. The two primary teachers are likely to determine policy by informal agreement while the head is acknowledged as the official leader by external groups and individuals. It may be appropriate to regard the management of such schools as comprising elements of both the collegial and formal models.

   In large and complex institutions, such as colleges and most secondary schools, there are numerous decision points leading to the development of alternative power centres. Staff may owe their first loyalty to their discipline and their department. These subunits compete for the resources they require to advance their objectives in a process encapsulated by the political model. In certain circumstances the situation may be so fluid that the ambiguity perspective appears to be appropriate.

2. *Organizational structure*   the nature of the organizational structure is likely to have a significant impact on school and college management. Heads who establish participative machinery may be motivated by a desire to involve professional colleagues in decision-making. The intention then is to create a collegial framework for policy formulation. However, the introduction of committees and working parties also provides several focal points for political behaviour. Interest groups seek representation on these bodies, engage in bargaining and attempt to build coalitions in order to secure favourable outcomes.

   The Pensnett school in Dudley illustrates the view that the collegial and political dimensions are both enhanced by the introduction of a participative structure. The committee structure became the setting for conflict between the academic and pastoral teams who were competing to establish the supremacy of their objectives (Bush 1989, p. 7).

   The formal model has limited validity where there is a participative structure, if the machinery is used for policy formulation and not simply to discuss the implementation of 'top-down' decisions.

3. *Time available for management*   the nature of the management process depends on the amount of time which participants are able and willing to devote to the wider organizational and managerial aspects of their work. In

the primary sector, teachers have full-time classroom responsibilities and only the head may be available to deal with management issues during the school day. This factor contributes to the limited influence of curriculum co-ordinators and prevents them from becoming alternative leaders. Campbell's (1985) research suggests that the lack of non-contact time is one of the main obstacles to the development of collegiality in primary schools. This problem may serve to reinforce the 'top-down' leadership style associated with the formal model.

In secondary schools and colleges, staff have periods of non-teaching time. The provision of this time for preparation and management is an important precondition for the development of collegial and political approaches. However, the extent to which committees enhance collegial decision-making may be influenced by the reluctance of staff to commit time for meetings. At Churchfields school in the West Midlands there were ample opportunities to participate within an elaborate committee structure but some teachers were unwilling to attend meetings (Bush, 1993). Where teachers opt out of committees and working parties they may be signalling their indifference to a participative approach. This tends to reduce the appropriateness of collegial and political perspectives and suggests the validity of the ambiguity model with its stress on fluid participation.

4. *The availability of resources*    the availability of resources is likely to play a part in determining the relevance of the various models. In periods of expansion it may be possible to adopt a rational approach to the distribution of resources or to rely on a collegial stance. When funding is limited, departments may face the possibility of reductions in real resources such as staff, books or equipment. In these circumstances, units are likely to seek to defend their interests. Committees and working parties may begin to resemble political arenas as subunits seek to retain existing resource levels. Davies and Morgan (1983, p. 164) chart the shift from formal and collegial approaches to a political perspective as budgets tighten:

> As long as powerful individuals and groups received what they perceived to be reasonable shares of expanding resources, the core organisational coalitions were maintained in relative harmony . . . As resources to meet the policy commitments and funding demands of competing organisational groups have diminished, institutional administrators have experienced an increased level of conflict.

5. *The external environment*    the external environment inevitably influences the process of management inside schools and colleges. The shift to a 'market economy' in education means that schools and colleges have to be responsive to signals from their environment if they are to thrive. Hoy and Miskel (1987, p. 103) stress the links between the environment and school management: 'The emergence of open-systems theory during the past two decades has highlighted the importance [of the] external environment on internal school structures and processes.'

In periods of relative stability, organizations may be able to adopt formal or collegial approaches. This may be true of institutions with good reputations; they may have an assured clientele and be insulated from environmental turbulence. Fluctuating levels of recruitment in many schools and colleges, however, lead to unpredictable funding with clear implications for staffing and other real resources. The ambiguity model is particularly salient in such an unstable climate.

While these issues are important determinants of structure and process, it is rarely appropriate to label any school or college as typifying a single model. Rather, elements of many or all of the models may be found in almost all organizations. The head of Churchfields school was right to claim that 'specimens of all the . . . models' (Bush, 1993, p. 41) could be found. In any one establishment, certain models may be more prevalent than the others but it is a question of relative not absolute significance.

This caution is important but it may be possible to conclude that small schools are likely to possess most of the characteristics of formal or collegial organizations, particularly in periods of stability. Large, multipurpose colleges undergoing rapid change may display many of the features of the political and ambiguity theories. Many secondary schools have elements of all these four models whose significance varies from time to time and with the nature of the activity and its participants. Adherents of the subjective and cultural models would add that much depends on the values, perceptions and interpretations of individuals and groups in the organization:

> Each set of models shades into the next because each model is necessarily partial . . . What is important will vary from one situation to the next, and from one observer or participant to another . . . Usefulness is not an objective criterion; it depends on the attitudes, values, beliefs, skills and experiences of the user.
>
> (Cuthbert, 1984, p. 62)

## Attempts at synthesis

Each of the six models discussed in this volume offers valid insights into the nature of management in schools and colleges. Yet all the perspectives are limited in that they do not give a complete picture of educational institutions. Rather they turn the spotlight on particular aspects of the organization and consequently leave other features in the shade. As we have seen, most educational institutions display features from most or all of the models: 'Any realistic approach to organizational analysis must start from the premise that organizations can be many things at one and the same time' (Morgan, 1986, p. 321).

The inadequacies of each theory, taken singly, have led to a search for a comprehensive model that integrates concepts to provide a coherent analytical framework. Ellstrom (1983, p. 236) makes the case for such a synthesis: 'Each model emphasises certain variables, while others are de-emphasised or ignored. Consequently, each model can be expected to give only partial understanding of the organisational reality. . . . it might be possible to obtain a more comprehensive understanding of organisations by integrating the . . . models into an overarching framework.' The attempt to develop coherence is not just a matter of esoteric interest for educational theorists. Chapman (1993, p. 212) stresses the need for leaders to develop this broader perspective in order to enhance organizational effectiveness: 'Visionary and creative leadership and effective management in education require a deliberate and conscious attempt at integration, enmeshment and coherence.'

Enderud (1980) and Davies and Morgan (1983) have developed integrative models incorporating ambiguity, political, collegial and formal perspectives. These syntheses are based on the assumption that policy formation proceeds through four distinct phases which all require adequate time if the decision is to be successful. Attempts by leaders to omit certain stages or to proceed too fast with initiatives may lead to a breakdown of the decision process or create the necessity for a 'loopback' to earlier phases.

These authors assume an initial period of high ambiguity as problems, solutions and participants interact at appropriate choice opportunities. This anarchic phase serves to identify the issues and acts as a preliminary sifting mechanism. If conducted properly it should lead to an initial coupling of problems with potential solutions.

The output of the ambiguous period is regarded as the input to the political phase. This stage is characterized by bargaining and negotiations and usually involves relatively few participants in small, closed committees. The outcome is likely to be a broad measure of agreement on possible solutions.

In the third collegial phase, the participants committed to the proposed solution attempt to persuade less active members to accept the compromise reached during the political stage. The solutions are tested against criteria of acceptability and feasibility and may result in minor changes. Eventually this process should lead to agreed policy outcomes and a degree of commitment to the decision.

The final phase is the formal or bureaucratic stage during which agreed policy may be subject to modification in the light of administrative considerations. The outcome of this period is a policy which is both legitimate and operationally satisfactory. The Davies and Morgan (1983) version of the model is shown as Figure 9.2.

Enderud (1980, p. 241) emphasizes that the significance of each phase varies according to the different perceptions of participants as well as the nature of the issue:

> With its four phases, the model . . . reflects a mix of different realities in . . . decision making – an anarchistic, a political, a collegial and a bureaucratic reality – which may all be part of any one joint decision process. This composite picture will be one of the reasons why different participants often can interpret the same decision as largely anarchic, political, collegial or bureaucratic, according to the phase which is most visible to them, because of their own participation or for other reasons.

Although Enderud acknowledges that the individual interpretations of participants may influence the visibility of the models, the subjective perspective is not featured explicitly in the syntheses discussed by him or by Davies and Morgan (1983). Theodossin (1983, p. 88), however, does link the subjective or phenomenological approach to the formal or systems model using an analytical continuum. He argues that a systems perspective is the most appropriate way of explaining national developments while individual and subunit activities may be understood best by utilizing the individual meanings of participants:

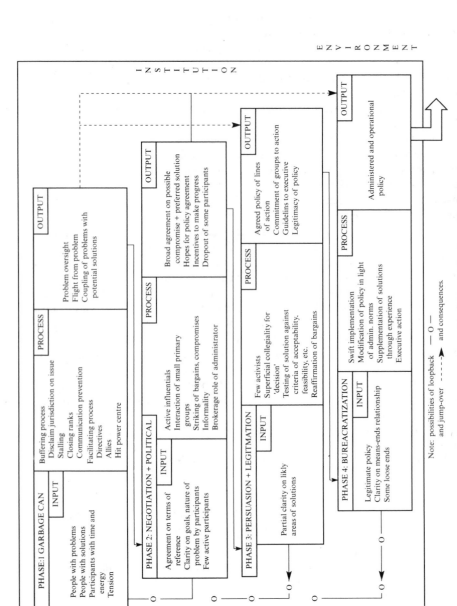

Asked to account for and to explain national movements . . . we are more likely to find that a systems perspective is an appropriate form of conceptual organisation: to think in terms of thousands of private biographies of the participating individuals is clearly to concern oneself with more detail than one can handle conceptually, let alone collect, and to segment the experience into an incoherent fragmentation. However, asked to explain the emergence of mixed-ability grouping in a particular school . . . we are likely to find the phenomenological approach more helpful: we are here dealing with change agents whose activities spring from personal, individual experience.

Theodossin's analysis is interesting and plausible. It helps to delineate the contribution of the formal and subjective models to educational management theory. In focusing on these two perspectives, however, it necessarily ignores the contribution of other approaches, including the cultural model which has not been incorporated into any of the syntheses applied to education.

The Enderud (1980), and Davies and Morgan (1983), models are valuable in suggesting a plausible sequential link between four of the major theories. However, it is certainly possible to postulate different sets of relationships between the models. For example, a collegial approach may become political as participants engage in conflict instead of seeking to achieve consensus.

## Using theory to improve practice

The six models present different approaches to the management of education and the syntheses indicate a few of the possible relationships between them. However, the ultimate test of theory is whether it improves practice. Theory which is arid and remote from practice will not improve school and college management or help to enhance teaching and learning, which should be at the heart of the educational process.

There should be little doubt about the *potential* for theory to inform practice. School and college managers generally engage in a process of implicit theorising in deciding how to formulate policy or respond to events. Morgan (1986, pp. 335–6) explains this process:

There is a close relationship between the way we think and the way we act . . . In using metaphor to understand organization we . . . are simply encouraged to learn how to think about situations from different standpoints. We are invited to do what we do naturally but to do so more consciously and broadly . . . Our images or metaphors *are* theories or conceptual frameworks. Practice is never theory-free, for it is always guided by an image of what one is trying to do. The real issue is whether or not we are aware of the theory guiding our action.

Theory provides the analytical basis for determining the response to events and helps in the interpretation of management information. Facts cannot simply be left to speak for themselves. They require the explanatory framework of theory in order to ascertain their real meaning.

The multiplicity of competing models means that no single theory is sufficient to guide practice. Rather, managers need to develop 'conceptual pluralism' (Bolman and Deal, 1984, p. 4) in order to be able to select the most appropriate approach to particular issues and avoid a unidimensional stance: 'Understanding organizations is nearly impossible when the manager is

unconsciously wed to a single, narrow perspective . . . Managers in all organ
izations . . . can increase their effectiveness and their freedom through the us
of multiple vantage points. To be locked into a single path is likely to produc
error and self-imprisonment.'

Conceptual pluralism is similar to the notion of contingency theory (Fiedler
1965) which stresses that the validity of each model varies according to th
context. Leaders should choose the theory most appropriate for the organiza
tion and for the particular situation under consideration. Appreciation of th
various approaches is the starting point for effective action. It provides a
'conceptual tool-kit' for the manager to deploy as appropriate in addressing
problems and developing strategy. The explicit acquisition of a range of the
oretical perspectives should lead to 'the wise manager making the most in
formed and appropriate selection of the multiple 'truths' available' (French
1989, p. 49).

This eclectic approach may be illustrated by reference to the task of chairin
a meeting. The chair may begin by adopting the normatively preferable col
legial model, particularly if there is a culture of collaboration in the school o
college. If consensus cannot be achieved, the chair may need to adopt th
political strategy of mediation to achieve a compromise. If the emerging out
come appears to contradict governing body policy, it may be necessary t
stress accountability, a central concept in the formal model. During the meet
ing, there may be different interpretations of the same phenomena and sen
sitivity may be required to this essentially subjective position. There may als
be elements of the ambiguity model, particularly if there is fluid participatio
in the discussion. Throughout the process, the chair may seek to ensure tha
the tone of the debate, and any policy proposals, are consistent with th
cultural norms of the organization.

Morgan (1986, p. 322) argues that organizational analysis based on thes
multiple perspectives comprises two elements:

- A diagnostic reading of the situation being investigated, using differen
  metaphors to identify or highlight key aspects of the situation.
- A critical evaluation of the significance of the different interpretations result
  ing from the diagnosis.

These skills are consistent with the concept of the 'reflective practitioner
whose managerial approach incorporates both good experience and a distilla
tion of theoretical models based on wide reading and discussion with both
academics and fellow practitioners. This combination of theory and practic
enables the leader to acquire the overview required for strategic management
Everard (1984, p. 17–18) suggest that this 'helicopter' quality is

> the statesmanlike attribute that enabled a manager easily to shift his [*sic*
> position between the particular and the general and abstract, so that h
> could relate seemingly unrelated experiences in his day-to-day work an
> make a coherent pattern of them (seeing both the wood and the trees an
> how they relate).

While it is widely recognized that appreciation of theory is likely to enhanc
practice, there remain relatively few published accounts of how the variou

models have been tested in school or college-based research. More empirical work is needed to enable judgements on the validity of the models to be made with confidence. As Bell (1984, p. 199) indicates, detailed observations are required to establish how decisions are made: 'These observations are the key to understanding those forces of power and influence, both inside and outside schools, which control and regulate them. Only in this way can the internal organisation of schools be fully understood.'

While observation is important, it may not be sufficient to judge the validity of the models: 'Empirical adequacy is not a sufficient criterion for deciding the merits of competing theories: the same empirical foundation may adequately confirm any number of different theories' (Evers and Lakomski, 1991, p. 101). Adherents of the subjective model would argue that observation is inadequate because it overlooks the perceptions of participants whose interpretations of events are central to any real understanding of educational institutions. Research is required which combines observation and participants' perceptions to provide a comprehensive analysis of school and college management. The objectives of such a research programme would be to test the validity of the models presented in this volume and to develop an overarching conceptual framework. It is a tough task but if awareness of theory helps to improve practice, as we have sought to demonstrate, then more rigorous theory should produce more effective practitioners and better schools and colleges.

# References

Baldridge, J. V., Curtis, D. V., Ecker, G. and Riley, G. L. (1978) *Policy Making and Effective Leadership*, Jossey Bass, San Francisco.

Bell, L. (1984) The sociology of school organisation: impossible or irrelevant?, *British Journal of Sociology of Education*, Vol. 5, no. 2, pp. 187–204.

Bolman, L. and Deal, T. (1984) *Modern Approaches to Understanding and Managing Organizations*, Jossey Bass, San Francisco.

Bush, T. (1989) School management structures – theory and practice, *Educational Management and Administration*, Vol. 17, no. 1, pp. 3–8.

Bush, T. (1993) *Exploring Collegiality: Theory and Practice, E326 Managing Schools: Challenge and Response*, The Open University, Milton Keynes.

Campbell, R. J. (1985), *Developing the Primary Curriculum*, Holt, Rinehart and Winston, London.

Chapman, J. (1993) Leadership, school-based decision-making and school effectiveness, in C. Dimmock (ed.) *School-based Management and School Effectiveness*, Routledge, London.

Cuthbert, R. (1984) *The Management Process, E324 Management in Post Compulsory Education, Block 3, Part 2*, Open University Press, Milton Keynes.

Davies, J. L. and Morgan, A. W. (1983) Management of higher education in a period of contraction and uncertainty, in O. Body-Barrett, T. Bush, J. Goodey, J. McNay and M. Preedy (eds.) *Approaches to Post School Management*, Harper and Row, London.

Ellstrom, P. E. (1983) Four faces of educational organisations, *Higher Education*, Vol. 12, pp. 231–41.

Enderud, J. (1980) Administrative leadership in organised anarchies, *International Journal of Institutional Management in Higher Education*, Vol. 4, no. 3, pp. 235–53.

Everard, K. B. (1984) *Management in Comprehensive Schools: What can be Learned from Industry?*, Centre for the Study of Comprehensive Schools, York.

Evers, C. and Lakomski, G. (1991) Educational administration as science: a post-positivist proposal, in P. Ribbins, R. Glatter, T. Simkins and L. Watson (eds.) *Developing Educational Leaders*, Longman, Harlow.

Fiedler, F. (1965) Engineer the job to fit the manager, *Harvard Business Review*, Sept-Oct.

French, B. (1989) *The Hidden Face of Organisations: Some Alternative Theories of Management*, Sheffield City Polytechnic, Sheffield.

Hoy, W. and Miskel, C. (1987) *Educational Administration: Theory, Research and Practice*, Random House, New York.

Morgan, G. (1986) *Images of Organization*, Sage, Newbury Park, California.

Theodossin, E. (1983) Theoretical perspectives on the management of planned educational change, *British Educational Research Journal*, Vol. 9, no. 1, pp. 81–90.

# Subject Index

# Author Index